D0855987

Life in Classical Athens

The Acropolis seen from the north-west

Life in
CLASSICAL ATHENS

T. B. L. WEBSTER
Drawings by Eva Wilson

B. T. BATSFORD LTD   London

First published 1969 (as *Everyday Life in Classical Athens*)
Reprinted 1978

Text © T. B. L. Webster, 1969
Illustrations © B. T. Batsford Ltd, 1969

Printed and bound in Great Britain by Butler & Tanner Ltd
Frome and London for the publishers
B. T. BATSFORD LTD
4 Fitzhardinge Street, London W1H 0AH

ISBN 0 7134 1279 8

PREFACE

In attempting to write this sketch of everyday life in Classical Athens I have interpreted Classical as meaning roughly from the time of the Persian Wars to the time of Alexander. I have no doubt that many important aspects of everyday life have escaped me through my ignorance or inadvertence. I felt that today classical Athenians are primarily interesting and important as having produced first-rate art and poetry, and that it was justifiable to conclude this book with an interpretation of their art and poetry because it pervaded their everyday life through public festivals, public buildings, and the minor arts. The first chapter gives geographical and historical background; the second and third give a general account of life at home and life in the City; the fourth and fifth describe the part played by religion and myth in Athenian life; the sixth tries to show the change of spirit evidenced by Athenian literature and art in the century and half of the classical period. I should like to acknowledge my debt to the excellent publications of the American excavations of the Agora, which was the hub of Athenian life. Mr P. Kemmis Betty has helped me very much in the choice of illustrations and Mrs Eva Wilson has converted many of them into excellent line drawings. I have not attempted to make my spelling of ancient names consistent.

T. B. L. Webster

ACKNOWLEDGMENT

The author and publishers would like to thank the following for the illustrations appearing in this book: the Acropolis Museum, Athens for fig. 85; Agora Excavation–American School of Classical Studies in Athens for figs. 34, 35, 76, 83 and 96; Alinari for fig. 32; Alison Frantz for figs. 5, 6, 37, 69, 75, 84, 86, 88 and 93; the Ashmolean Museum for fig. 20; the Trustees of the British Museum for figs. 7, 52, 70, 73, 74, 81 and 99; the City of Birmingham Museum and Art Gallery for fig. 53; A. F. Kersting for figs. 26, 40, 41 and 79; the Mansell Collection for figs. 72 and 94; Museo Municipale, Lecce for fig. 67; the Metropolitan Museum of Art, New York for fig. 80; the Museum of Fine Arts, Boston, Mass. for fig. 65; the National Museum, Copenhagen for fig. 18; and the Staatliche Museen zu Berlin for fig. 89.

CONTENTS

THE ILLUSTRATIONS

8

9

CHRONOLOGY

LITERATURE AND THOUGHT	BIRTH DATES

<table>
<tr><td></td><td>525 Aeschylus</td></tr>
<tr><td></td><td>522 Pindar</td></tr>
</table>

500-400 B.C.	Tragedy, Comedy, Sophists, Historians and early orators	500/490 Anaxagoras Sophocles 490/480 Herodotos Euripides Protagoras 469 Sokrates

c. 460 Thucydides

458	Aeschylus, *Oresteia*	
443	Sophocles, *Antigone*	c. 450 Aristophanes
431	Euripides, *Medea*	436 Isokrates
429	Sophocles, *Oedipus Tyrannus*	427 Plato
428	Euripides, *Hippolytus*	
425	Aristophanes, *Acharnians*	
415	Euripides, *Trojan Trilogy*	
407	Euripides, *Bacchae*	
406	Sophocles, *Oedipus Coloneus*	
405	Aristophanes, *Frogs*	

400–300 B.C.	Plato: Lysias and Isokrates: Aristotle Middle and New Comedy	

387	Foundation of Plato's Academy	384 Aristotle Demosthenes 373 Theophrastos

367/47 Aristotle at the Academy

347	Death of Plato	
335/322	Aristotle at the Lyceum	342 Menander
332/287	Theophrastos at the Lyceum	
321	Menander's first production	

CHRONOLOGY

ART	HISTORY

From 530 B.C.
Red figure style in Attic vase painting

Temple of Aphaia at Aegina   Persian Wars 490–480

Temple of Zeus at
Olympia 460

                Periclean rule 460–430

Parthenon 440/30

                Peloponnesian War, 431–404

Nike temple, Erechtheion   Peace of Nikias 421
420/10

                Sicilian Expedition 415-13

                362 Battle of Mantinea

About 350   360/338 Philip of Macedon
Praxiteles'   338 Battle of Chaeronea
Hermes
Demeter of Knidos   338/323 Alexander of Macedon

I

Background

Everyday life in classical Athens was very different from everyday life in a modern city. One has to think away city conveniences such as cars, railways, aeroplanes, washing machines, gas, electricity, central sanitation, main water supply, elaborate health services, postal services, newspapers, gramophones, radio, television and many other things, like combine harvesters in the country, that we now take for granted. Some can remember a time before the First World War when many of these necessities were known only to the rich in the larger cities; some will know places today where many or all of these things are lacking.

The essentials of everyday life have not changed; children are born and grow up, they have to be fed and dressed and educated, they go out into the world, marry, have careers, they play some part in politics, and if they are unlucky are sent to war, they have leisure which they use for physical or mental enjoyment, they stand in some relation to the supernatural, and this relation determines their belief in what will happen to them when they die.

Modern science has certainly altered our religion. This revolution had already, as we shall see, begun in ancient times, indeed before our period opens. But the thought that the world works like a machine takes a long time to penetrate all parts of the human mind. We are far readier than the Greeks to attribute natural events to natural causes. We still have harvest festivals, but we put more trust in rotation of crops, fertilisers, weed-killers and combines than in the gods who preside over weather and agriculture. To understand the Greeks we have to think ourselves back to a much more primitive way of looking at things; almost every operation—sowing or ploughing, a new baby, a commercial venture—would be preceded by a vow to a god and, if successful, followed by an offering to the gods. It is not so much our attitude to the supernatural that has changed as the range of events which we now control by purely human endeavour.

Modern technology has made life in some ways safer, since our expectation of life is much greater, in some ways easier, since we spend less time ourselves on collecting and preparing food and making clothes and long journeys, and to a great extent machines can do for us what in the past we caused other human beings to do; we no longer need so many servants or slaves to do for us what we do not want to do ourselves. But it is probably true that the human brain cannot send or receive more signals in a day than before. Modern technology partly saves time on routine so that more time remains for meaningful action, partly increases our range so that what we do may affect the other side of the world, and so that we can see and hear what goes on on the other side of the world.

The growth of science and technology has both made possible and has demanded an immense complication of life. We pursue a large number of highly specialised careers which build up the complex structures of modern industries, professions, educational establishments and government. We have to think ourselves back into a much simpler form of life. There were a few quite simple basic trades; the manufacturers and their retailers operated in the same 25 acres of Athens, the Agora or market-square, which held most of the offices of government and many temples and shrines. All that could be produced at home was produced at home. Professions like the law and medicine existed, but on the whole the citizen knew his own law and there were no hospitals, no anaesthetics, and only such drugs as could be obtained from herbs. Within their limits doctors were highly skilled in observation and diagnosis, were among the greatest scientists of their day, and had a highly developed professional conscience. Universities did not exist, and the startling advances which the Greeks made in science and philosophy were made by private individuals and discussed at meetings in private houses or at the gymnasium in the intervals of athletic exercise. Organised entertainment in our sense did not exist, but the frequent religious celebrations, private and public, gave enough opportunity for poets and musicians to perform, and when the gods demanded so many gifts in return for benefits the artist probably had more chance of getting large or small commissions than he has today. As a whole, society was far more integrated than it is today. The gap between the richest and the poorest was far smaller; with so little specialisation everybody knew more about everybody else's job, the separation between manual and white-collar worker did not exist; artist and poet filled a real religious and social need; even the slaves were much less cut off from their fellow man than the very poor in an affluent society. Without modern systems of communication a large population could not be effectively governed. When the fourth-century political philosophers, Plato and Aristotle, limited the size of an ideal city to something like 10,000 adult males, they were thinking partly of effective control and partly of effective response from the citizens. A considerable portion of the citizens of Athens probably did attend the Assembly, did know Perikles and the opposition speakers by sight; now television, radio and newspapers can establish communication of this kind between rulers and ruled in a state with a population more than a thousand times as large. But the members of the modern state only take direct part in government when there is an election or more rarely when there is a referendum. But the Athenian Assembly (or ekklesia) had ordinary meetings four times a month and extraordinary meetings for emergencies. Every citizen could attend, but with a number of citizens away on military or naval service and a number living too far off to come in except for very special business, an attendance of 5,000 or a fifth of the citizen body was probably good. Nevertheless, the policy of Athens could be decided at these public meetings, and although the measures put before the Assembly had been previously scrutinised by the Council, the decision was in the hands of the Assembly, and the great debates on foreign affairs, like the discussion in 415 BC as to whether to send an expedition to conquer Sicily, took place in the Assembly, and every citizen who attended felt that he had taken part.

Without modern technology man has to aid him in communications only hands and feet, writing (but not typing or printing), horses and mules and sailing ships. For an effective democracy classical Athens with a population of about 25,000 adult male citizens and a territory which formed an isosceles triangle with sea on two sides (its base is about 50 miles long from Salamis in the south to Rhamnous in the north, and its length about 50 miles from Phyle in the west to Sounion in the east) was probably about

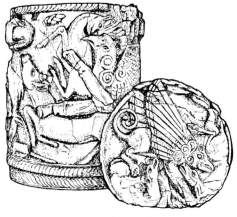

2   Mycenaean ivory ointment box

as large as could work under ancient conditions.

By classical Athens we mean Athens and the surrounding territory called Attica between 480 and 330 B C. What goes before is called Archaic Athens, what comes after is called Hellenistic Athens. The bottom date is given by the conquests of Alexander the Great: this meant on the one hand an immense extension of the Greek world to include Egypt and much of Asia, but on the other hand a corresponding decrease in the importance of the old city-state of the Greek mainland. Athens remained as an immensely respected centre of literature, art, and thought; politically it was nominally free, but actually always open to attack or patronage from one or other of the Hellenistic kings descended from the generals of Alexander, with whom the real power lay, until they in their turn succumbed to Rome.

Athens was one of the great Mycenaean centres, as the considerable Mycenaean remains in Attica and Athens itself show (2). The Acropolis hill, five miles from the sea, protected behind by its ring of mountains, was a typical Mycenaean site, and there is probably some truth in the legends of Theseus centralising the government of Attica in Athens and of Theseus slaying the Minotaur and so preventing Attica from paying tribute to Crete.

Much later, some 60 years after the Trojan War, Athens accepted a king who had been driven out from Pylos by the invading Dorians, and the last of their Pylian kings, Kodros, died defending the Acropolis successfully against a Dorian attack. From that time Athens had no kings; the kingship was replaced by three officials called archons, one civil, one religious and one military. The civil archon was called the eponymous archon because the year was dated by him: 'in the archonship of X'. The religious archon was called the king archon because he took over all

BACKGROUND

religious functions of the king. The military archon was called the Polemarch. The government was still in the hands of the great families and they held office at first for life, but subsequently for ten years, and finally the archonship became an annual office. The ex-archons passed into the Council of the Areopagos, which was both a murder-court and a powerful conservative brake on reform. This was the beginning of the political development which led to democracy in the classical period. Two important later stages are the reforms of Solon at the very beginning of the sixth century BC, which gave even the poorest Athenian citizen a vote in the Assembly and a chance to serve as a juryman, and after the long interlude of the Peisistratos' tyranny the reforms of Kleisthenes towards the end of the sixth century, which established a division of Attica for political and administrative purposes into 170 demes or parishes. These ran their own religious and secular affairs and sent representatives to the Council of Five Hundred which prepared the business for the Athenian Assembly. For higher administrative purposes the demes were grouped in 30 trittyes, ten composed of city demes, ten of inland demes, ten of coastal demes, and the 30 trittyes in ten phylai or tribes, so that each tribe contained one city, one coastal and one inland trittys. An Athenian's official name consisted of three parts: his own name, his father's name in the genitive, and an adjective derived from the name of his deme. Kleisthenes also introduced ostracism, the possibility of expelling a prominent citizen for ten years if sufficient votes were registered against him.

The subsequent historical developments belong to our period: in 462 BC the Areopagos was stripped of all its guardian functions and reduced to being a murder-court; in 457 the archonship, which had previously been occupied by the top two property classes, was opened to the third of the four property classes; soon after this Perikles introduced payment for jurymen, which made it very much easier for the poor citizen to serve; pay for attendance at the Assembly was not introduced until the early fourth century.

Let us look for a moment at some of Kleisthenes' demes in their geographic setting, and ask what memories their demesmen might have (3). The triangular territory of Athens is bounded by the sea on two sides and on the west by the neighbouring states of Megara to the south and Boeotia to the north, with whom relations are sometimes good and sometimes bad. Across the Boeotian border

17

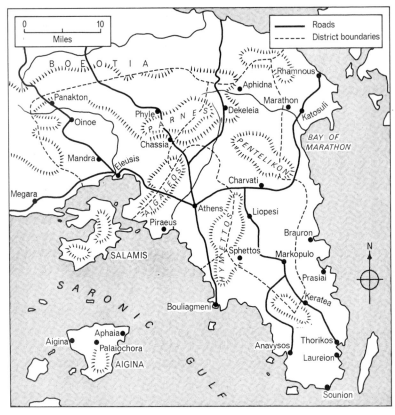

3 Map of Attica

north of Megara was the great mountain of Kithairon where the
child Oidipous was exposed in the hope that he would not kill his
father, and Pentheus was torn to pieces by his mother Agave,
subjects of classical Athenian tragedy. Below it was Plataiai, where
the final great land battle was fought against the Persians in 479,
and Eleutherai with a cult of Dionysos, which was brought to
Athens about 600; it was in honour of this god that tragedy, satyr
play and comedy were performed.

South of Eleutherai on the coast was the deme of Eleusis with its
very ancient shrine of the goddesses Demeter and Persephone, who
had sent Triptolemos out to teach the world agriculture; here the
mysteries were celebrated, which promised their initiates a better

life after death. The bay of Eleusis is almost blocked by the island of Salamis, and in their narrow waters the sea battle against the Persians was fought in 480. The possession of this island was long disputed between Megara and Athens, and it was finally won for Athens by Solon's efforts in the early sixth century and became an Attic deme: the great Homeric hero of Salamis was Ajax. The north-east end of Salamis nearly reaches across to the Peiraeus, the harbour of Athens with naval arsenals and dockyards. Here towards the end of the fifth century the Syracusan Kephalos lived, in whose house Sokrates had the great discussion recorded by Plato in the *Republic*. Kephalos was a rich resident alien who owned a considerable shield factory. One of his sons was Lysias, who became a professional speech writer after the family fortunes had been plundered by the Thirty Tyrants, a brutal conservative oligarchy who ruled Athens at the end of the Peloponnesian War, 404–403, and put to death, among many others, Lysias' brother Polemarchos, the young man who first debates with Sokrates in the *Republic*. These resident aliens (metics) paid taxes and did military service but could not hold office; they were welcome because they were usually skilled craftsmen. The Peiraeus was a great international port and had therefore many foreign cults. It has been suggested that the very enlightened idea, held by some of the most advanced thinkers in the fifth century, that race and social status are artificial barriers to the essential unity of mankind, owed a great deal to the mixing of nationalities in this cosmopolitan port.

The bays at the Peiraeus made good harbours for both merchant ships and warships. Merchant ships proceeded for the most part by sail alone. Warships had oars as well as sails—the typical Athenian warship was the trireme, which had its rowers arranged on three steps running the length of the ship with the highest step and the longest oars in the centre. Each trireme carried 174 oarsmen, ten marines, a steersman, and a boatswain to give the time to the oarsmen. The captain or trierarch was a rich man appointed by the state to keep the trireme in running repair for a year; he could appoint a deputy to sail the ship. In the fifth century the Athenian navy was the sea police of the Athenian empire, which extended over the whole Aegean, and its defence against Persian or other fleets.

East of Kithairon is the Attic range of Parnes, which guards the

4 Marble girl
from Brauron

north-western side of Attica. The fort of Phyle is built to protect the road through the pass from the frontier, and there many young Athenians (ephebes) did their second year of military service. The deme centre is a little way from the fort. Above the deme centre in a difficult patch of mountain side is a cave, where Pan and the Nymphs were worshipped for centuries: this hard rugged country was the setting for a comedy produced by Menander in 316, the *Dyskolos* or *Grumpy*. The text of this play was first published in 1959 and was our first example of an Athenian social comedy of the late fourth century. It belongs just outside our period but gives a good idea of the hard life of an Attic farmer in the mountains; this has not changed, and the olive trees, the pear trees, the wild thyme, and the rocks are still there today.

Rather further to the east in the foothills of Parnes is the deme of Acharnai. In 425 the comic poet Aristophanes made the chorus of his *Acharnians* charcoal-burners of Acharnai and they give a vivid picture of the tough, conservative Attic countryman. The plain below the foothills was good agricultural land, and the deme put a large number of heavy infantrymen (hoplites) in the field in 431 at the beginning of the Peloponnesian War. A very fine beehive tomb, containing pieces of boar's tusk helmets and of lyres decorated with ivory plates, shows that there must have been a considerable Mycenaean settlement here; the tomb had a cult which was celebrated from the eighth century into classical times. We do not know what the hero was called, but he was evidently regarded as a powerful force to be propitiated.

About ten miles to the north-east was the deme of Aphidna, which sent a line of politicians with a definite policy to the city in the fourth century. Here a ruined Mycenaean fort has been found, and suggests that some historical struggle lies behind the legend that Theseus carried off Helen from Sparta and hid her at Aphidna, until her brothers, the Dioskouroi, Kastor and Polydeukes, fought Theseus there and brought her home.

From Aphidna it is less than ten miles to Marathon on the east coast, where the great battle with the Persians was fought in 490. The grave mound where the dead were buried still stands, and it is today extraordinarily moving to see, in the Benaki Museum in Athens, an arrowhead picked up on the field of battle. In the hills above Marathon there is a cave of Pan which was a cult place from Neolithic to Mycenaean times, and the cult was revived in the fifth century: Pan had appeared in 490 BC to Philippides when he took the news of the Persian invasion to Sparta, and demanded worship from the Athenians, which they duly gave him.

Further south on the east coast are the two neighbouring demes of Brauron and Halai Araphenides. Brauron had a large and fairly early Mycenaean house and a temple of Artemis. She was served by little girls called Arktoi (bears), and they lived in the precincts of the temple until they married. This is obviously a very old and strange cult. In the ruins of the fifth-century temple charming statues of the 'bear' girls have been found (4). At Halai Araphenides was another cult of Artemis, who was there called Tauropolos; 'tamer of bulls' was the real meaning of the name for this ancient goddess of wild-life, but the name was interpreted as Queen of the Tauroi in the Crimea, and her statue was said to have been brought from there; according to Euripides it was brought by Orestes and Iphigeneia, who was her priestess and was

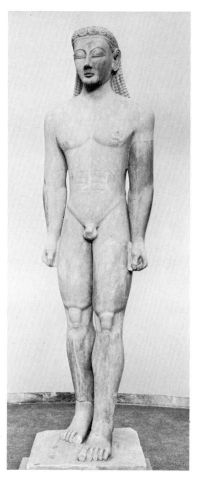

5 Kouros from Sounion, 600 BC

finally buried at Halai and worshipped in a shrine by the temple.

The southernmost tip of Attica belonged to the deme of Sounion. The cape was crowned by the magnificent fifth-century temple of Poseidon, the first sight a sailor saw as he returned to Attica from across the Aegean. In its precincts was found an over-lifesize statue of a young male (5), one of the earliest known Attic statues, and fragments of at least three others. They were not statues of the god, but dedications. One theory was that the god would be pleased if he were given a servant of stone, who was more durable than a living servant. These are male parallels to the many marble girls (korai), dedicated to Athena on the Acropolis.

Just behind Sounion were the silver mines of Laureion which had been worked since the eighth century. A great strike was made about 483 and the surplus was used to build the fleet which in 480 defeated the Persians at Salamis. The state leased the mines to private citizens, who employed slaves in large numbers to extract the silver from the workings: they undoubtedly had the worst life of anybody in what was, on the whole, a tolerant and benevolent society.

Round Cape Sounion and a little way back from the coast was the deme of Aigilia, which grew the finest figs in Attica. It is remarkable that five magnificent grave monuments have been discovered there, dating from the beginning of the sixth century to the beginning of the fifth; four of them are young naked males, and the fifth a very beautiful large relief with a boy and a girl. Some great family must have lived there, and this celebrated their dead. A clue has recently been seen in the inscription carved on the base of one of the male statues (6): 'Stop and pity Kroisos as you pass by his tomb, whom once fierce Ares destroyed in the front line.' The young Athenian who died in battle about 540 was called Kroisos after the famous king of Lydia. One great Athenian family had connections with King Kroisos, the Alkmaionidai, to one of whom Kroisos had given as much gold as he could carry in return for help at Delphi. He might well have named his son after their benefactor. The boy must have been a contemporary and a relation of Kleisthenes, who made the system of demes. In our period the most famous of the Alkmaionidai was Perikles.

This rapid survey may have given some idea of the variety of this tiny country, of the wealth of legend and history which the classical Athenian knew. The starting point of classical Athens is the battle of Salamis in 480. We must go back to Kodros and the eleventh century for a moment to understand Athens' peculiar importance in this struggle. Kodros' sons led the migration which settled the Greek cities on the sea-board of Asia Minor. The reason may have been overcrowding, since Athens seems to have been one of the great centres where refugees from the Dorian invasion sought safety. Certainly these people seeking new homes across the Aegean had memories of earlier Mycenaean settlements in Asia Minor. After a long struggle with the Asiatic inhabitants the new cities flourished, Miletos, Ephesos and the rest, and developed art, literature and thought on their own lines. When the Persians conquered Kroisos of Lydia soon after the middle of the sixth century, they went on to subdue the Greek cities. The Greek cities revolted in 500 and sought help from Athens. The help was ineffective, but showed Dareios, King of Persia, that if he was to control the Greek cities of Asia Minor, he would also have to control at least Athens in mainland Greece. He made the attempt with a naval expedition in 490, which the Athenians defeated when it put in at Marathon. Ten years later Dareios' son, Xerxes, mounted a more formidable expedition by land and sea, and the Greek city-states, with a few exceptions, united to block it. The Spartans fought with desperate

6   Kroisos from Aigilia, 540 BC

23

valour at Thermopylai but could not stop the land army which overran Athens. The Athenians managed to force a naval engagement off Salamis, and this was so successful that the Persian fleet and the army returned with Xerxes to Asia, leaving an experienced commander and a picked force to finish off the rebellious Greeks. This force was resoundingly defeated by the Spartans at Plataiai in 479.

The Persian wars were for the Greeks the unique historical event which immediately became a myth of heroic size, as, in later years, were the Spanish Armada and the Battle of Britain for the English and the landing at Gallipoli for the Australians and New Zealanders. In the Greek case, at any rate, the reality was very different from the myth and much less heroic. There were squabbles and treacheries, and probably the Persians were not really so overwhelmingly efficient as they appeared to their antagonists. These blemishes on the picture did not matter because what survived was the memory of an heroic event, the belief that a small number of brave men fighting for the principle of democracy did battle with a powerful and ruthless autocratic despot and succeeded against overwhelming odds. It is therefore true to say that, although the reality was much less heroic than the myth and although many of the new tendencies can be traced back before 480, the Persian wars crystallised in the minds of the Greeks a new feeling that they were a united nation, a new codification of the relation between gods and men, and a new realisation of the responsibility of the individual. Of course the Greeks were not united, and the history of the fifth century is to a large extent the history of a prolonged struggle between Athens and Sparta. It is nevertheless true that the multitudinous Greek city-states were for the most part collected into two major unities, one dominated by Athens and one dominated by Sparta, and it is also true that all Greeks felt themselves to be Greeks and not barbarians. This is the new situation which makes 480 a reasonable date for starting a description of classical Athens.

In what follows we shall only be concerned marginally with the external and internal history of Attica. The first half of the fifth century is succinctly summed up by the historian Thucydides; the alliance of Greek states against Persia became a domination by Athens and the domination became an Athenian empire. By the middle of the century the members of the original alliance were paying tribute to Athens, sending offerings to Athenian festivals, and having certain lawsuits tried in Athens; in return the Aegean was policed by the Athenian navy, but they had to face the probability of Athenian interference in their politics if they adopted a form of government unfavourable to Athens. Athens became the central market of the Mediterranean, and Perikles (7) certainly had the conception of making his rebuilt Acropolis 'an education to Greece' and the capital of the empire. Certainly this tribute of the allies contributed to the beautification of Athens, but Athens was not economically dependent on the tribute, as she continued to prosper in the fourth century after the collapse of the empire. Sparta and the other Peloponnesian states, particularly Corinth, grew increasingly afraid of the growth of Athenian power, and a major war broke out in 431 and lasted for ten years until an inconclusive peace was made. Then in 415 the Athenians madly tried to conquer Sicily and suffered a resounding defeat. Even then it took another 12 years and the internal revolution of the Thirty Tyrants before the Spartans were able to conquer Athens. The peace-terms were generous and Athens soon recovered. Neither the Spartans, at the beginning of the fourth century, nor the Thebans rather later, succeeded in dominating Greece. It was only when the Macedonians first under Philip, and then under Alexander conquered successively mainland Greece, the Greek islands and then

7 Perikles

25

Asia and Egypt, that the whole balance changed and the Hellenistic kingdoms were formed.

War was not total war; there was a definite campaigning season. The Peloponnesian War was certainly uncomfortable; the yearly invasion of Attica damaged land and property, and many Athenians were on service at home and abroad and suffered casualties, but everyday life went on and the magnificent series of tragedies and comedies, sculptures and paintings produced during the last 30 years of the fifth century is evidence of its quality.

Our concern is with this everyday life, how the Athenians lived at home and how they were educated, how they lived in the city and pursued their private and public lives, how they worshipped their gods, how at different times and on different occasions they thought of their heroes, how their art and literature changed with the changing climate of thought from the time of the Persian War until the rise of the Macedonians.

2

Life at home

Modern novels contain many detailed descriptions of the houses used by the characters. In Athenian literature the references are only incidental, and we have to add to them what we can find from excavations and what we see in the way of household equipment from the pictures on vases. One source deserves special mention. Shortly before the sailing of the Athenian expedition to Sicily in 415, Alkibiades and a number of others were accused of parodying the Eleusinian Mysteries in a private house near the Agora and of damaging the phallic images of Hermes (called Herms) which stood in front of many houses and in public places in Athens. Information was given as to the perpetrators, they were exiled, and their property auctioned by the state auctioneers (poletai) for the benefit of Demeter, the goddess of the Mysteries; the accounts of the sales survive partly in an ancient lexicographer, partly on the original marble slabs on which they were inscribed —known as the Attic Stelai. Even in their present damaged and fragmentary state they give a precious record of the property owned by well-to-do Athenians in 415.

Athenian houses normally consisted of a courtyard entered by a passage from the street; rooms were built on all sides of the courtyard with doors opening on to it, and probably on one side the house had an upper storey where the sleeping quarters were. This upper storey never survives, but occasionally traces of stairs have been found, and references to upper rooms in literature are common. The walls were usually built of mud-brick on a stone base and the roof was tiled.

Houses varied, of course, greatly in size. Three may be taken as examples. The smallest of the three is the house of a cobbler, which was close to the boundary stone of the Agora, and was built

27

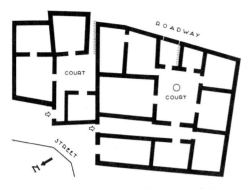

8 Private houses to the west of the
Areopagos

before the Persian Wars. When the Persians sacked Athens they apparently bundled everything down the well in the courtyard. The family (or another family) rebuilt and re-occupied the house after the war, and dug a new well in the courtyard. The courtyard was only 18 by 21 feet, but there was room for a lean-to against the north wall, and here were found numbers of hobnails and eyelets for laces. So the owner was a cobbler. A wine jar of the late sixth century, now in Oxford, shows a cobbler sitting in his shop with a boy standing on his table having the soles of a pair of shoes cut out while his father looks on. A lucky chance preserved, in the house in the Agora, the foot of a drinking cup with the name Simon scratched on the bottom. Literature tells of a cobbler called Simon, with whom Perikles and Sokrates used to go and converse. He took notes of Sokrates' conversations and wrote them up afterwards in dialogue form. There is no reason why he should not have been the owner of this house.

A larger house about a quarter of a mile south-west at the bottom of the west slope of the Areopagos also contained a work-shop or shop, but this shop was cut off from the rest of the house and had its own door on the street so that the occupant may have had nothing to do with the householder. This house had, besides the separate shop, nine rooms opening on to the courtyard (*8*). Of these the biggest, measuring about 20 by 15 feet, was the men's dining room (andron), and a rather smaller room opposite it was shown by the number of loom-weights and spindle-wheels found in it to be the room where the women did their spinning and weaving. Two adjacent small rooms were kitchen and bathroom.

The same general ground-floor plan appeared again in a large country house at the foot of the north slope of Mount Aigaleos: there the andron was $16\frac{1}{2}$ by $15\frac{1}{2}$ feet and would take seven couches for diners. The courtyard was 30 by 36 feet and had on one side a large room with central pillar and no front wall, which was perhaps meant for animals or as a store for agricultural implements. The bathroom was next to it, right away from the main line of rooms: the room next to the andron is interpreted as a 'living kitchen', then a room with a hearth in it, then a large double room where the women did their spinning and weaving.

The house was apparently occupied for a fairly short time of peace between the two stages of the Peloponnesian War, roughly 422–413, so that what was found in it indicates the normal non-perishable equipment of a largish country house. We can compare it with the lists from the auction to see what is missing, and the objects can be illustrated from Greek vases.

In both the country house and the Areopagos house the bathroom was identified by a drain leading outside the house and a terracotta bath, rather like the old-fashioned hip-bath in shape. The water would be brought from the well in the courtyard and, if desired, could be heated on the way. In Menander's *Dyskolos*, the well is almost a character in the play: first, the old woman drops the bucket down the well (it is not a bucket, but a round clay jar called a kados, which can be seen in many pictures); then she tries to get it out with her master's mattock and drops the mattock in too; finally the old man tries to get it out and he slips on some dung in the courtyard (presumably he kept animals in his courtyard) and falls in himself. He had probably been too mean to protect his well with a well-head or a wall, like the one on the vase illustrated, to prevent such accidents (9). To let down a kados on the end of a rope was the normal way of getting water, but some wells had the bucket attached to a counter-weighted beam swinging on a post (known as keloneion). Ordinary washing was done at basins on a stand: the country house had a rather elaborate one made of stone (probably the one listed in the auction-lists was similar)

9 Woman at well

10   Women washing

as well as a more ordinary one of terra-cotta. A woman on a vase has a kind of mop, presumably a stick with a sponge on the end, with which she is washing herself (*10*).

After washing, men rubbed themselves with olive oil and women with perfumed oil or perfumed ointment. Two ointment pots were found in the large country house, but perhaps the country was not a place for much beautification. The auction-lists give six alabastoi, which were certainly designed for perfume. The name is interesting and means 'made of alabaster', but these pots were almost certainly made of clay. Quite early, in the seventh century, the Greeks had imported alabaster vases of perfume from the East. Then they started making their own perfume by adding herbs to olive oil. But the name of the bottles was still used for locally made clay copies of the same shape.

The cook who had been hired for a wedding in one of Menander's comedies asks whether the kitchen is roofed or not; presumably the cooking was often done in the courtyard, but a room with a hearth, like the one in the country house, would need a chimney (in Aristophanes' *Wasps* the young man has to put a beam on the top of the chimney to prevent his father escaping). Cooking was often done on a small portable hearth (eschara), and the country house had a number of casseroles with lids, and the all-purpose chytra or rough jug with wide mouth, which was used for heating water or soup or vegetables (*11*). Roasting and baking were done in small clay ovens.

The auction-lists give some idea of normal stores. They include barley, wheat, millet, lentils for soup, coriander and sesame for seasoning, grapes, figs, olives, almonds for dessert, olive oil, wine and vinegar (it is curious that the famous Attic honey is lacking, but bees are included under livestock). The country house had remains of five large pithoi, the enormous storage jars which would be sunk in the ground and which have remained unchanged in shape and construction from Minoan Crete to the present day. Liquids (and other things that were not needed in large quantities) were kept in rough two-handled jars (stamnoi or amphorae), and the country house had one wine amphora imported from the island of Chios. The auction-lists give both Chian and Eretrian amphorae, and a number of large shallow basins, both round and bath-shaped (skaphai).

It is surprising to find even in the country house that they drank wine imported across the Aegean from Chios as well as wine grown on the farm. But we have evidence from several sources including comedy about the number of imports into Athens in the fifth century. Although Attic wine was exported, luxury wine was imported from Lesbos, Chios and Thasos. Other imports were woollen textiles from Miletos, flax (needed for sails as well as clothes) from Egypt and Asia Minor, and especially corn from the Black Sea. A fourth-century figure shows that Attica produced only a third of the corn consumed and the other two-thirds were imported. This explains the need for policing the Aegean and the need for friendly Greek cities on the route leading to the Black Sea. The exports were wine, oil, honey, scent, pottery, and above all silver, which came not only from Laureion but also from the north-eastern part of the Athenian empire. The historian Thucydides drew an income from a silver mine in Thrace. The Athenians paid for much of their imports in silver, and within the Empire much of the silver was returned to them in the form of tribute paid for their services in policing the Aegean.

The grain in the auction-lists shows that bread-making was usually done at home, and the country house had a quern. The grain was ground by the women: the method was to rub a stone quern backwards and forwards in a wide shallow trough (kardapos). Rotary mills were apparently

11 Cooking pots

12   Fish-plate

unknown. The ordinary mortar stood quite high off the ground, and was operated with long pestles.

Otherwise the chief items of food were vegetables, eggs and fowls (poultry could be kept in the courtyard, and cocks could be trained for fighting), and fish. No place in Attica was very far from the sea on one side or the other, and Mediterranean fish are plentiful and varied in size and flavour. They could be eaten fresh or salted and kept in jars. In the fourth century charming plates were produced with a depression in the middle for sauce and pictures of fish on the flat part (*12*).

Something was added to the larder by hunting. A detailed treatise by Xenophon describes ancient hunting. It is good to see that cultivated land and particularly growing crops are to be avoided. Hounds should be given short names so that they will respond to them willingly. Prayer is to be offered to Artemis and Apollo before the hunt, and they are to be given their share of the game afterwards. Three types of game are mentioned: hare, deer and wild boar. For each, as nowadays, different kinds of hounds were used. Hare-hunting and deer-hunting is a two-man business. The huntsman takes with him a net-keeper, if he is hunting hare, and his weapon is the club. For hunting deer he has a hound-master, and he uses javelins and traps. Boars are much more dangerous, and larger parties were needed, equipped with spears, javelins and nets. Xenophon is concerned to defend hunting as a training in the art of war, and implies that it is a rich man's sport. In Menander's *Dyskolos* it is the rich farmer's son who goes hunting in the country round Phyle, and he hunts with a single slave, who is presumably his net-setter.

Country houses kept animals: oxen for ploughing, pigs for lard and bacon, sheep for wool, goats for milk and cheese, mules for baggage. Meat was eaten only on special occasions, generally either on the festival of a god, when the animal was cooked and sacrificed to the god and then divided up among the worshippers, or at a great private occasion like a wedding. The whole family would be present at a sacrifice and any guests that the master or son of the house would invite. The altar in the courtyard would be used for the sacrifice if the meal was at home. Poor men in the city might club together (eranos) to buy themselves an animal to sacrifice, and so get their Sunday joint. Most families seem to have hired a professional to cook meat, and the word mageiros means both butcher and cook: they brought their cooking pots with them, which they either owned or hired in the Agora. Mageiroi are stock figures in comedy and gave themselves tremendous airs about their skill in carving and cooking.

As today olive oil was used largely in cooking. Attic olives were very good, and the oil was widely exported. It was used for lighting and for rubbing on the body after washing and exercise, and it was the basis for perfumes. The olive tree was the gift of the goddess Athena to her favourite city, and the first olive tree grew on the Acropolis. The Persians cut it down in 480, and when they departed it miraculously sprouted again. The state had a register of the sacred olive trees which were supposed to be descended from the original olive tree. Their oil was requisitioned by the eponymous archon (the chief civil official) and kept on the Acropolis until the time of the great Panathenaic festival, which was celebrated every four years. When the time came the oil was handed over to the officials of the games, who had already had something like 1,000 amphorae made, with a picture of Athena on one side and of an athletic contest or chariot-race on the other. They were the prizes for those who won in track events or chariot-races: 100 of them are listed in the auction-lists, and it is possible that they were the prizes won by Alkibiades in the chariot-race in 418.

The country house probably had its own olive trees. Surplus oil (and other produce, including animals) would be taken into Athens to market. But home consumption for all the various needs must have been considerable. Lighting was done by small round glazed clay lamps with a spout for the wick (*13*). They gave a

13   Lamps

33

surprisingly good light, better than a candle. Some of them were made with a hole through the middle so that a number of them could be put one on top of the other on a lampstand (lampstands are among the items in the auction-lists), and larger lamps had a number of spouts for wicks. Richer houses had similar lamps of bronze or even silver. Probably in the country at any rate people went to bed soon after sunset and got up before dawn so that not much illumination was needed. But drinking parties (symposia) went on far into the night, and in the city lamps were needed also to find the way home at night or for those going out to keep an early morning engagement, such as jury service. The flame might be protected by a wicker shield or even enclosed in a lantern with horn sides.

The two chief rooms in the house were the loom-room and the men's dining room or andron. The loom-room was probably where the women spent most of their waking time and received their guests. The whole process of making textiles was done here, except perhaps the preliminary washing of the fleeces, which would be done in the courtyard. Even in the city most women seem to have bought the wool straight from the sheep; and, of course, the more prosperous had land in the country with sheep, oxen and goats, as well as town houses. The auction-lists give one man who had a town house, two country houses on the coast, and two estates inland (one at Aphidna).

The washed fleeces were beaten on a bench to get out impurities, and then straightened out on the bare legs of the women into hanks for spinning, and were then put into a basket. There was a special leg-shield which could be worn for this; they were made of terracotta and sometimes beautifully decorated. One made about 450 has an exquisite picture of the marriage of Alkestis and was surely a wedding-present. The picture shows a special type of wedding-vase, one of which was found in the country house; in origin it was the cauldron to heat the water for the marriage-bath, but these are quite small and are used to hold flowers.

The hanks were then spun. The wool was put on the distaff and the thread was pulled out by the spindle; the spindle was weighted with the whorls, which are found so commonly in excavations of ancient houses and often show which room was the loom-room. The women could stand or sit to spin. When they sat, they either sat on chairs with a curving back (anaklisis, in the auction-list) or on a four-legged backless stool (diphros). The pets of the house might visit them, a dog, or a cock, or a crane. The ordinary loom was a large wooden frame with the threads hanging and weighted, and the wooden shuttle with the horizontal thread was thrown across from one side

14 Loom

to the other (*14*). The weaving was pushed up tight with a rod.

The wool was often dyed red, yellow, black, blue or green; and the decoration was woven in (embroidery in the technical sense did not exist in the classical period). There were also tiny looms which could be held on the knee for small fine pieces of fabric. The patterns were the traditional patterns known from Greek buildings and Greek vases: key-pattern, battlements, rose-buds, lotus-flowers and palmettes. But in the latter part of the fifth century, particularly, scenes from mythology and fabulous animals were often included; this was called 'barbarian weaving', and the fashion for such elaborate textiles came from the East, but the designs were purely Greek. Besides wool, the Greeks also used linen for the garment which they wore next to the skin, knee-length for boys and young men, full length for older men and women; and countrymen wore leather jerkins. But the standard textile was wool of various thickness and weaves. The rectangular piece of woven wool served as cloak, wrap, blanket or curtain according to its size, thickness or design. The textiles were kept in wooden chests which might be veneered with other woods, or decorated with inlay of ivory, or fitted with corners and feet of bronze.

The other chief room was the andron or men's room, where they had their meals and their drinking party (symposion) after dinner (*15*). During the day they were mostly out of the house—working on the land, looking after the animals, overseeing their workers or doing local business at the deme headquarters, if the

35

15 Symposion

house was in the country, or doing private or public business in the market-place (Agora) or elsewhere in Athens. In spite of the absence of transport Greeks did not worry much about distances. Countrymen often came into Athens or went down to the harbour at the Peiraeus. Undoubtedly the time-schedules of comedy do not work out in real life, but the general notion that the father of the family in the country went into the Agora to do business or down to the Peiraeus to see whether his ship had come in, if he owned a ship, cannot be wholly unrealistic.

Probably also when the men were at home the courtyard was a natural place to collect and talk. The andron did not hold a great deal more than the couches on which the diners reclined. The andron in the country house was planned to take seven couches round the walls. The normal size of couches was five feet two inches long by two feet six inches wide, so that they would not leave much wall space in a room $16\frac{1}{2}$ by $15\frac{1}{2}$ feet. The Greeks did not have cupboards, but they did have a piece of furniture called a kylikeion, a kind of dresser, on which cups and statuettes could be put, and there would be one of these opposite the door. Cups and jugs were often hung on the walls, and the nails could also take basket-work bags, when the guests brought their own food with them, and bottles of perfumed oil. Flowers, too, were a necessity. The diners wore wreaths round their heads, originally in honour of the god to whom the animal had been sacrificed or in honour of Dionysos as the god of wine. Wreaths were hung on the walls, and sometimes long streamers of vine or ivy. In richer houses the walls might be painted, usually with blocks of plain colour to look like masonry, often leaving a frieze at the top which might be decorated with painted wreaths or ivy. Alkibiades employed a first-rate painter to decorate his house, and he, as we shall see, did something more elaborate. Textiles could be hung on the walls, and this was probably where the parapetasma or curtain in the auction-lists came from. Mosaic floors began to be made in the late fifth century and they copied the designs of textiles: Greeks thought textiles too precious for the floor.

The couches themselves were the same as the beds used for sleeping (*15*). The framework was carved and decorated. One end was raised to take cushions, and they were covered with woven and patterned blankets and rugs. A table was put before each couch, usually three-legged with an oblong top, but they also had round tables with four legs. The food was served in the dishes from the kitchen, and no implements seem to have been used except knives. Sauces, salt, and the like were served in small bowls.

What we call Greek vases are largely drinking vessels and scent-bottles or ointment pots. Greeks always drank their wine mixed with water; they needed, therefore, water-pots, ladles, mixing-bowls and jugs, as well as wine-bottles and cups. The water-pots (hydriai) had two handles at the sides, so that they could be lifted easily on to the head (there are many pictures of women walking from the fountain-house with hydriai on their heads), and a handle at the back for pouring. The mixing-bowl (krater) must be large and have a wide mouth so that when the wine is mixed it could be extracted in ladles or small jugs (oinochoe) for pouring into the cups. Cups are of two main kinds, deep and stemless (skyphos), and wide and shallow with a stem and foot (kylix). The large kylixes are beautiful in shape, and not so difficult to drink out of as they appear, because the lip is not quite flat but raised slightly where you drink. Both kinds of cup have firm horizontal handles so that they can be used for flicking dregs on to a mark. This is the game called kottabos. There were several variants. One was to try and sink small saucers floating in a bowl; another was to bring down a counterweighted scale so that it hit the head of a little figure on a stand.

There were four main sorts of pot decoration in our period: one way was to cover the visible surfaces of the pot with shiny black glaze and impress little formal designs on the glaze with stamps. The second was to use the same black glaze as a background and leave the figures and objects in the red colour of the clay with inner markings done in the same black glaze, either thick or diluted so as to be semi-transparent. This is called red-figure: the reverse process, known as black-figure, was to leave the background unpainted and paint the figures in black on the red clay, doing the inner markings with an incised line, which cuts through the glaze, and adding red and white for details on top of the black glaze. This technique had nearly gone out in 480, but survived on the special amphorae given as prizes at the Panathenaic games (29), an understandable piece of conservatism, like the picture of an old-fashioned warrior Athena on one side of these pots. The fourth technique was to cover the body of the vase with a slip of fine white clay and paint on that in outline and colours: this technique was chiefly used for vases made to hold perfume offered to the dead. The drawing is often lovely and we shall have more to say about it later.

The quality of potting and painting of red-figure vases was also extremely good. The range of subjects painted gives some idea of the taste of the Athenians who bought them. First, they had a very wide knowledge of mythology and were interested in a large number of mythological scenes; sometimes we can say that the introduction of a scene in vase-painting follows pretty quickly on the production of a tragedy on the same theme in the theatre. Secondly, they were interested in every kind of daily life, from the most intimate scenes of the bedroom to the activities of soldiers, fishermen, huntsmen and craftsmen. Thirdly, the style of the drawing changes fast and was parallel to contemporary large-scale painting: so evidently the artistic tastes of the purchasers changed quickly too.

It is important to establish this. Not only does the swift change of style make it possible to date works of art to within ten years during our period or at any rate down to about 375, but the swift reflection of changes in the style of the major arts of sculpture and painting in the minor arts of pottery, statuettes of bronze and terracotta, silver ware, jewellery and coinage, must mean that there was extraordinarily little resistance to these changes: patrons

16   Silver cup

of art at all levels were prepared to commission or buy the latest thing as soon as it appeared. Whether the patron was Perikles commissioning Pheidias to make the cult-statue for the new temple on the Acropolis or a victorious athlete commissioning a sculptor to make a portrait-statue to celebrate his victory, or a boy giving his girl a scent-bottle, they all wanted the latest thing. The conservatives criticised Perikles' building programme, but that criticism was political and not aesthetic. Plato, as we shall see, criticised the emotionalism and illusionism of late fifth-century art, but this criticism was partly ethical, partly metaphysical, and not aesthetic. As far as we can see, public taste was with the artist in an extremely rapid advance.

The country house had only two red-figure vases (in addition to the special wedding-vase mentioned above). The cups were all of the cheaper black-glaze ware impressed with palmettes. On the other hand, references in literature and a single entry in the auction-lists suggests that the rich normally used bronze or silver vessels for table service, like the very beautiful silver cup with the moon-goddess (Selene), which was found in Bulgaria (*16*). Besides pictures of potteries there is a good mid-fifth-century red-figure hydria showing a workshop in which four young men and a girl are decorating metal vases of various shapes (*17*). They are visited

17   Metal-workers

in their shop by two winged Victories (Nikai) and the goddess
Athena, so that they were evidently successful.

A number of people who rated between the rich and the owners
of the country house more than provided the market for ready-
made red-figure vases, whether they wanted them for household
ware or as dedications to a god in return for a benefit bestowed
or expected, or as presents for friends or relations, or as prizes in
minor competitions (the inscription on the base of one black-
figure cup shows that it was given as a prize in a competition of
girls in carding wool).

But we have to suppose that quite a lot of vases were made to
special orders for special occasions and then were sold off and
found their way by the second-hand market to Etruria or wherever
outside Greece they were finally discovered. The same painter
who painted one of the two mixing-bowls in the country house
produced two mixing-bowls which can fairly be called special
orders: one has a picture of a poet called Phrynichos, a flute-
player, and a chorus of singers performing (*18*). The figures are
all named and three of them are names known to us. This vase
must have been painted to celebrate a victory with a particular
choral song in Athens, but the vase was found in Italy. The other

has a picture of the sacrifice of a sheep: again the figures are named and are known, including Plato's notorious uncle the tyrant Kritias, the leader of the Thirty Tyrants at the end of the Peloponnesian War. This may even have been painted for a party celebrating the formation of a political conspiracy, but it was found in Capua and the Campanians can have had no knowledge of the occasion. Of course such special vases might be kept by their owners: thus an amphora of the special Panathenaic shape found in the Athenian Agora has a picture of three young men with names inscribed moving past an olive tree, one of them carrying a Panathenaic amphora—this evidently celebrated the occasion when the special amphorae were brought to the Acropolis to be filled with the special oil as prizes in the next festival, and its owner preserved it.

Sometimes then we can suppose that special drinking vessels were ordered for a symposion which followed a dinner given to celebrate a special occasion (*15*). The symposion described in Plato's dialogue of that name was at the house of the tragic poet Agathon two days after he had produced a successful tragedy. The

18 Dithyramb singers

night before he had had the victory feast (with a sacrifice and therefore meat) and a great crowd attended: as it is described as a feast for 'himself and his chorusmen', a special mixing-bowl like the Phrynichos vase would have been exactly in place. On the second night special friends were invited; the dialogue names seven people, so that the dining room of the country house would have been the right size. Evidently Agathon's room had only seven couches, as when Alkibiades, drunk and supported by a flute-girl, arrives in the middle of the discussion, room is made for him to sit between Agathon and Sokrates: he does not recline but sits on the end of Sokrates' couch.

Here the entertainment during the drinking (Sokrates stays outside until the eating is over) is speeches made by each of the guests in praise of Love. Alkibiades' entrance is only a momentary diversion, and the last speech is Sokrates' highly philosophic speech. But Alkibiades' entry explains many of the pictures of young men roaming the streets with a flute-girl and holding cups: they are going from party to party like Alkibiades. Alkibiades is wearing a wreath of ivy and violets (probably in honour of Dionysos) and has long ribbons (tainiai) in his hair, some of which he ties round Agathon's head, as they were traditionally worn by victors.

Alkibiades' flute-girl takes no further part in the proceedings. Normally she would have entertained the guests, and many pictures of symposia show girls with flutes, lyres or harps sitting on the ends of the young men's couches or standing as they play. They were accompanists rather than singers themselves. We also hear of jesters, jugglers, girls doing sword-dances, girl acrobats, and even a sort of ballet as entertainment at symposia. These girl-entertainers were usually slaves and very often non-Athenian, who brought their masters an income by being hired for the evening. They were trained in musical schools, which young men used to visit to the distress of their elders. They were attractive and the young men fell in love with them, and often kept them for a longer or shorter time as mistresses. Full legal marriage was impossible, because the law forbade an Athenian to marry a non-Athenian, but certainly in the fourth century a young man could treat such a girl as his wife and recognise her children as his legal heirs; in fact a new kind of marriage, a love-match with a foreigner, was becoming more common.

The songs sung at symposia were sometimes short skolia, stanzas of four lines, which the drinkers would sing in turn. Often they were political and the most famous is the song which celebrated the murder of the tyrant Hipparchos and therefore the origin of Kleisthenes' democracy: 'With my myrtle wreath, I'll wear my sword, like Harmodios and Aristogeiton, when they killed the tyrant and gave Athens equality'. But often the drinkers sang high poetry. When the elderly rustic hero of Aristophanes' *Clouds* goes to a symposion with his son, he asks him to take the lyre and sing an ode by Simonides celebrating an athletic victory or some Aeschylus, but the boy insisted on singing (or reciting to accompaniment) a speech from the latest play of Euripides. In a similar scene in Aristophanes' *Banqueters* the father asks for a drinking-song of Alkaios or Anakreon. What is interesting is both the time-range and the variety. Those two plays of Aristophanes were written in 427 and 423. It is true that revivals of Aeschylus kept his memory alive, but Simonides was born in 550, Anakreon about 560, and Alkaios lived before 600, and a young man was expected to be able to sing not only drinking-songs of long ago but also victor-odes and tragedy. They must have had a considerable education in poetry and music. So the singers and their accompanists lead us into two elements of everyday life which we have as yet scarcely touched: the position of slaves and the education of the young.

Because slavery has been (nominally at least) abolished in the modern world and because we are accustomed to free labour (however badly the poorer members of our society may suffer), it is easy to decry the ancient Greeks as a society based on slave-labour. Two obvious points must be made at the outset. No ancient society did without slaves, and therefore it is unhistorical to taunt the Athenians with having slaves. Secondly, the Athenians treated their slaves better than any other ancient society. Bound up with the works of Xenophon is a fascinating document which seems to be a political tract written just before the Peloponnesian War to

19 Slave from comedy

convince the Spartans that, however lax and undisciplined Athenian society might seem, they would fight for their ideals, and part of the argument is that the lack of subservience in Athenian slaves, which shocks a Spartan, has a perfectly sound theory behind it: Athens needs a mobile labour force both for the navy in times of crisis and for industry. The source of labour is the slaves, who are owned by Athenian citizens: the owner must have an incentive to lend his slave to the state or to someone else who requires labour; the slave must have an incentive to work when he is not under his master's eye. The slave is therefore paid, and in his turn pays a proportion of his wages to his master; that provides an incentive for his master, but the slave keeps a proportion of his wages for himself with which he can ultimately buy his freedom. And he has a certain amount of security because, if he is robbed or otherwise wronged, his master can go to law for him; this security was necessary if the slave was to work for wages away from home. We have several references to the practice in literature. The man who informed against the conspirators who mutilated the Herms in 415 claimed that he had seen them by moonlight in the theatre of Dionysos when he was on his way to Laureion to collect the wages of his slave. In Menander's *Epitretontes*, the charcoal-burner comes to his master's house to pay the rake-off from his wages. An extreme case of going to law for a slave is in Plato's *Euthypron*: Euthypron is suing his own father for the alleged murder of a slave through neglect.

One class of slave, then, is the wage-earning slave who has some hope of buying his freedom. The hopes of the mine-workers at Laureion were probably minimal; the hopes of the flute-girls and harpists who played in society must have been very high. Between those lie a large number of craftsmen, whose hopes cannot have been too low. We meet them in the auction-lists: goldsmith, fabric-maker, spit-maker, cobbler, donkey-driver. Most of them are foreigners and seem to have learned their trades in Athens. On the job they apparently got the normal wages for an Athenian citizen; at any rate in the accounts for the Erechtheion all the sculptors were paid a drachma a day whether they were slaves or free. To give a modern money equivalent is impossible, but it perhaps helps to say that it is three times as much as the daily allowance to a juryman. The average price of the slaves in the auction-lists is 174 drachmai, but the goldsmith fetched

360 drachmai. This gives some idea of the possibilities of buying freedom: a skilled craftsman would be paid a drachma a day and would be allowed to keep one-sixth of a drachma for himself. The fourth-century slave Pasion became a banker, and when he died left a large fortune, including an armaments factory, but presumably not many slaves were as successful as he.

The auction-lists also give three slaves classed as 'born in the house'; probably they were generally the children of the men and women slaves in the household and became in their turn the slaves of the sons and daughters of the house. Sometimes probably the father was the master of the house or his son, but in fact we hear very little of this. It is difficult to get any accurate figures but the general impression from literature and inscriptions is that the only people who owned large numbers of slaves were those who owned wage-earning slaves, whether they hired them out to the state or other private individuals or whether they worked directly for him. The conservative statesman and general Nikias had 1,000 slaves working the silver mines, and the orator Lysias had 120 slaves in the shield-factory. In the auction-lists Kephisodoros, who was a resident-alien in the Peiraeus, owned 16 slaves, and this sounds like a workshop, but we cannot tell of what kind. Adeimantos had six slaves, including a spit-maker and two cobblers: one of the cobblers had property of his own which was sold up with the rest, so that he was on the way to freedom.

We know from comedy that the Athenian household used a certain amount of free labour. The son of a poor neighbour might work for wages on the land, and the daughter help the mistress of the house with the wool-work. The children's nurse would be a slave and might be kept on

20   Sail-chariots

45

after they grew up, or go with a daughter to her new house when she married. A male slave might look after the son of the house, take him to school and to the gymnasium. He was called a paidagogos, and when the boy was older, the slave might be very helpful in getting money out of his father to meet his youthful extravagancies. But the vast majority of Athenian households seem to have been quite small.

The child's early years were spent in the home. Several vases show a baby in a high chair made of terracotta, and an actual example discovered in the Agora was arranged to have a chamber-pot underneath. The child had its toys: tops, jointed dolls, hobby-horses. In Aristophanes' *Clouds* the father speaks with pride of his son: 'you can't think how clever he was making houses and ships and wagons and frogs out of bits of leather'. He might have a pet dog. A bit later he would raise hares, like the boy on a cup in London (*59*), or pit his cock against a neighbour's cock. And there was a game like hockey, and another ball-game rather like pelotte. A novel kind of racing is illustrated on a very pretty oil-bottle painted about 490 (*20*). Two boys have little chariots which are drawn by branches of what look like fir: they are in fact sail-chariots. (The oil-bottle itself was carried hanging from a broad leather strap around the wrist so that after exercise the boy would always freshen himself by rubbing on some oil, and the excess

21–2   School

46

would be taken off with the curved bronze scraper called a strigil.)

Much preliminary education must have been done in the home by parents, nurse and paidagogos. We have little in detail about schools (although they certainly existed before our period began), but we know three names of professional educators: paidotribes or physical-trainer, grammatistes or writing-master, kitharistes or instructor in the lyre. A number of terracottas of the late fourth century represent an elderly man showing a child a writing-tablet; he looks like a slave and probably the grammatistes usually was a slave, and therefore a foreigner. This would be one way of accounting for the strange misspelling on a number of school slates found in a school near Plato's Academy and dated to the end of the fifth century. The school-master was teaching the children to spell proper names wrong.

The kitharistes primarily taught the lyre as his name implies, but music for a Greek did not exist apart from poetry and dancing, so that the school of the kitharistes was one of the sources of the range and variety of poetic knowledge that the young men showed in their symposia. A cup, painted by the vase-painter Douris about 480, gives a good idea of the kitharistes school (*21*). Cups, lyres, a flute-case, a papyrus roll, a curious basket with feet (perhaps meant for carrying papyrus rolls) are hanging on the wall. On the left an elderly man is seated with a lyre and a boy sits opposite him,

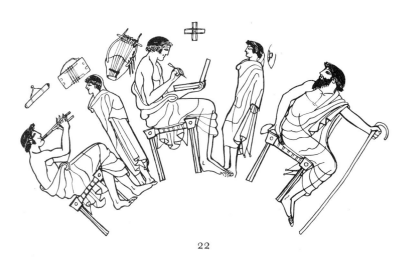

22

also with a lyre; the boy is presumably being taught a song by the old man. In the middle an old man is seated with a papyrus roll on which a line of hexameter verse, the beginning of an epic, is written: the boy standing beside him is evidently reciting the epic. On the right a man is watching; he is probably the paidagogos, the tutor-slave who has brought the two boys to school.

Another watcher like him appears on the other side of the cup (22). The two seated teachers are quite young; one plays the flute, and perhaps the standing boy is singing to his accompaniment. The other has a writing-tablet and a stylus on his knee; it looks as if he were correcting the standing boy's exercise. If so, this school combined the functions of the grammatistes and the kitharistes, and the boys learned writing and reading as well as playing and singing and recitation.

We always think of poetry as something on a printed page which, if we read it at all, we read with the eye, and we seldom hear it aloud except when somebody else, *not* the poet, sets it to music. For classical Greeks poetry was always something to be heard, and the papyrus roll was a memory-aid for recitation or singing rather than a text to read. They distinguished between spoken poetry, poetry recited to an accompaniment, and sung poetry. But the distinction was one of degree rather than of kind, and in the classical period no musical composer is ever named apart from the poet. Very little is known about classical Greek music. Probably it was extremely traditional and in the main emphasised the rhythm, except in so far as a professional accompanist, particularly a flautist (for they were highly esteemed and highly paid), wove arabesques round it. The important thing was the rhythm, the beautifully precise, elaborate and readily intelligible metrical system, into which the poet cast his words and which defined the dance-steps of the chorus if he was writing a choral ode; and to judge from the

23   Kithara-singer

pictures even a solo-singer did not stand still, but the rhythm communicated itself to his whole body (23). So the training with the kitharistes was a training in the peculiarly Greek combination of poetry, music and dancing, and the boys not only became acquainted with past and present poetry, which they would later sing or hear at the symposion, or store as treasures in their memory, but also acquired the technique for performing new sung and danced poetry on the many religious or semi-religious occasions when it might be necessary.

The paidotribes was concerned with physical-training, and his work led on to preparation for the various athletic contests, which included a Boys' Class as well as a Men's Class. The age limit for the Boys' Class was 18 years, because after that the boy was enrolled on the deme register and became officially an Ephebos; as an Ephebos, he did his two years of military training, after which he was in the Men's Class for contests. The paidotribes probably took his pupils in either a palaistra (wrestling school), or a gymnasium (training ground). The palaistra was called after the man who owned it. In the classical period there were three gymnasia all outside the city walls and all associated with a hero or god—the Academy associated with the hero Akademos, the Lyceum associated with Apollo, and Kynosarges associated with Herakles. Both palaistra and gymnasium catered primarily for athletics and had tracks for running, sometimes covered, sometimes in the open (the Academy had a grove of sacred olive trees); they had various sanded areas for boxing, wrestling, long-jumping (in which the Greeks always held jumping weights), javelin-throwing, both ordinary javelins and the javelin with a thong which sent it in a spin, and diskos-throwing; they also had a room with benches for undressing, and washing arrangements which might include besides ordinary basins in niches, a plunging-pool and a steam- or sweat-bath.

The washing arrangements were very like the arrangements in the public-baths. The best known is probably the Serangeion at the Peiraeus, which was functioning before 422. It was built partly in natural caves which were sacred to the hero Serangos (his name simply means tunnel). It had a plunge-bath, basins, a sweat-bath, and a room for anointing oneself, which had on the floor a very early pebble mosaic with a chariot driven by a woman across the sea. One curious difference between the public-baths on the one hand, and the palaistra and gymnasium on the other, was that the baths were despised as a place where the young wasted time gossiping, but the palaistrai and gymnasia were famous as places for philosophical discussions.

The older men went down to see the boys and young men exercise, and obviously there was a good deal of sitting about between events, and the undressing-rooms with their benches were convenient places to sit, and the covered tracks and plantations were convenient places to stroll. Sokrates, in his ceaseless endeavour to define moral virtue, used both palaistrai and gymnasia as places for meeting and talking to young men, and the Sophists used to display their skill in argument there, as well as in the houses of the rich, probably because they were good places for advertising themselves and attracting pupils. Later, in the fourth century, Plato started his philosophical school by making a shrine of the Muses in the Academy gymnasium, and Aristotle later still started his philosophical school in the Lyceum gymnasium. So although their purpose was primarily athletic, the palaistrai and gymnasia also served for higher education, and were the nearest thing that the Greeks had to a university. In the Hellenistic period gymnasia normally had lecture-rooms and even libraries as part of their buildings.

In our period higher education was by modern standards extremely haphazard. It is true that the ordinary Athenian saw nine tragedies every year at the City Dionysia, and in Aristophanes' *Frogs* it is accepted doctrine that the object of the tragic poet is to educate his audience. Whether the poets themselves so conceived their art is perhaps not so certain, but tragedies produced for an audience of 14,000 clearly had an enormous popular impact and what they meant in terms of ideals and ideas will be discussed further in the last chapter. But higher education in science, politics or philosophy was extremely haphazard. In the first place none of the early practitioners were Athenians. The scientific revolution began in the Greek city of Miletos in Asia Minor very early in the sixth century; however much they owed to earlier poetic cosmogonies the philsophers of Miletos tried to explain the world in terms of processes known in everyday life. The primary scientific problem at the next stage was to make such explanations cogent by developing the technique of argument so as to give scientific-philosophical argument something of the rigorousness of mathematical argument: this, I think, was the scientific importance of Pythagoras, Herakleitos and Xenophanes, although they themselves would probably have rated much more highly what we should call their ethics and metaphysics, and it is only their new conception of a self-sufficient, omnipotent god and their new conception of an immortal responsible soul, which comes into everyday life at the beginning of our period through the works of poets and dramatists.

We think of mathematicians, scientists, doctors, political theorists, moral philosophers, communications-experts, historians and poets as belonging to separate and usually mutually exclusive categories, which may or may not be covered by any one university umbrella. In the fifth century the brilliant men embraced at least two of these departments: Alkmaion of Kroton, doctor, mathematician and political scientist; Anaxagoras of Klazomenai, natural scientist and metaphysician; Diogenes of Apollonia, doctor and metaphysician; Protagoras of Abdera combined cosmogony, history of culture, political theory, theory of argument and grammar; Prodikos of Keos combined metaphysics and semantics; the Eleatics combined metaphysics, mathematics and technique of argument; Sokrates turned from natural science to ethics and technique of argument. With this wholesale overlapping it is wrong to think of doctors, mathematicians, sophists and philosophers as belonging in different boxes. The division of learning was only beginning; but it was beginning, and in particular mathematicians and medical scientists split off on their own, and teachers of communication and rhetoric split off on their own.

Anaxagoras, Diogenes of Apollonia, Protagoras and Prodikos visited Athens for shorter or longer periods in the fifth century, and Sokrates was an Athenian. But how much did they contribute to higher education? All except Sokrates wrote books, but these must have had a tiny circulation among friends. (Euripides, who owned one of the first private libraries, lent his Herakleitos to Sokrates.) The Sophists, Protagoras, Prodikos and the rest gave lectures in rich men's houses and took a few pupils for high fees. Sokrates wrote nothing, but talked to all and sundry, and had a few devoted aristocratic pupils. The two historians, Herodotos, who lectured in Athens in 445 and died in the early 420s, and Thucydides, whose work was published perhaps early in the fourth century, were in very different ways imbued with the new thought, and their books must have done something to disseminate the new ideas in so far as they affected history. But apart from conversation and the symposion, which must never be underrated, drama was perhaps the chief method of communication: the comic poets caricatured modern ideas, and the tragic poets were influenced by them in interpreting traditional mythology. Drama was seen by every Athenian and it is therefore in discussing drama that a little more will have to be said on this subject.

In the fourth century the situation changed. The circulation of books was much easier (and both Plato and Aristotle meant their dialogues for a wider public than their immediate adherents), and the philosophical and rhetorical schools began. Not too much must be read into the large word schools. The rhetoricians Lysias and Isokrates used their own houses, as far as we know; Plato used the Academy gymnasium but also the house which he bought close to it. All three were small establishments with a small number of pupils, but pupils of considerable stature. Only the briefest of sketches is possible here. Both Lysias and Isokrates lost their money in the Peloponnesian War and set up as teachers: Lysias was primarily a writer of speeches for clients in the law-courts and a teacher of practical rhetoric. Isokrates, besides teaching practical rhetoric, had a wider aim: he wanted his pupils to be able to influence politics by an informed view of Athens' past greatness expressed in ornate prose, and he sought successive solutions to the problem of Greek disunity, finally looking towards Macedonia. His pupils included statesmen and poets as well as orators.

Plato's solution was fundamentally different: in modern terms we should perhaps say that he believed in a rigorous training in mathematics as a preliminary to a metaphysic which enabled the pupil to derive the principles of practical government from the Idea of the Good, perceived through this training as the principle of the Universe. This is the purest and most uncompromising position which Plato publicised in the *Republic*; it produced as a sideline virulent criticism of art and literature which will occupy us later. From 367 the direction changed, partly owing to the practical needs of pupils, partly because of the arrival of distinguished foreign researchers, most of all, I suspect, because of the arrival of the young Aristotle, who was basically an empirical scientist rather than an idealist philosopher. From now the Academy was concerned with rhetoric, literary criticism (in a new positive form), scientific classification and logic, as well as mathematics and pure philosophy, and it is this tradition of science and scholarship which Aristotle developed when he returned to Athens in 337.

The impact on everyday life of all this was small. Plato and Aristotle did have some effect on political life, and the effect becomes clear in the Hellenistic age (pp. 173f). Their literary and artistic criticism, as I hope to show below, both influenced and was influenced by Athenian literary and artistic practice, and so they had an effect on what the ordinary Athenian saw and heard. The Academy can justly be termed the beginning of organised Higher Education, and so this brief account was necessary. But the beginning was small, and I do not think it was unfair to say that higher education in our period was haphazard. The young man picked up what came his way in discussions in the gymnasia, of which the Academy was one, and in the Agora, and he was exposed annually to performances of tragedy and comedy at the Dionysiac festivals.

After this education, and after his two years military training, the young man might think of setting up house on his own, or bringing his wife into his father's house. How much chance he had in practice of choosing his wife for a legal marriage is impossible to say. Formally, at any rate, his father arranged the marriage with the father of the bride and they agreed on the dowry and trousseau that the bride should have. The bride was prepared by a bridesmaid and the bridegroom had a best man. Both were bathed in water from a special holy spring: we have already noted the special vases used on this occasion. A wedding meal was held in the bride's house. The bridegroom then fetched her to her new home. The marriage song was sung on the way by the young friends of the pair, and there was further singing outside when they went into their bedroom. So a new cycle of life was begun.

3

The city

Athens is dominated by the Acropolis with the theatre of Dionysos nestling in its south-eastern slopes and next it the Odeion, which was a concert hall (they will occupy us when considering religion, festivities, art and literature). To the south-east was the great and unfinished temple of Olympian Zeus and the gymnasium of Kynosarges; the Lyceum lay to the east and the Academy to the north-west. Immediately under the north-west end of the Acropolis was the Agora (24) which will chiefly concern us in this chapter. It was bounded on the west by the hill on which the temple of Hephaistos (long called the Theseum) stood and on the south-west by the Areopagos. Here the council of ex-archons sat, the council of the Areopagos. In the period immediately after the Persian Wars, they were, according to Aristotle, the government of Athens, because of their immense authority derived from the fact that they had provided the money which made it possible to fight the sea-battle at Salamis. In 462, after a series of prosecutions of individual members, they lost their wider powers and became simply a murder-court. In 458 Aeschylus in the *Eumenides* put on the stage the establishment of the Areopagos, the first murder-court, established to try Orestes for the murder of his mother, Klytaimnestra. It is a fair conclusion that Aeschylus wanted them to be seen as a murder-court, a very venerable murder-court, not as a kind of powerful Upper House. Some 500 years later it was on the Areopagos that St Paul preached to the Athenians.

Between these two hills the way led on south-west to a third hill, the Pnyx (32), where the Athenian Assembly (ekklesia) met. The Panathenaic Way, along which the great procession in honour of Athena went every fourth year, ran down north from the Acropolis and diagonally north-west across the Agora and out to the Dipylon

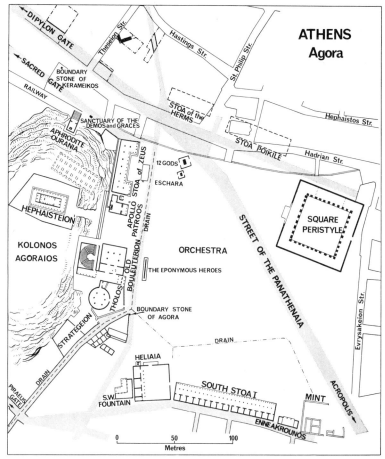

24   Plan of Agora

gate. The house in which the Mysteries were parodied (see p. 27) was on this road between the boundary of the Agora and the Dipylon gate. From the Dipylon gate three roads led: one south to the Peiraeus, one, 'the Sacred Way', west to Eleusis, one north to the Academy.

The platform from which funeral orations were delivered for those killed in war, including the famous funeral oration of Perikles reported by Thucydides, was just outside the gate, and in our period the chief cemeteries of Athens were in this area along the 'Sacred Way' and the road to the Academy. In the first half of the fifth century the tombs were marked by a simple marble slab with a sculptured palmette, but from the late fifth on to the last quarter of the fourth century, elaborate grave reliefs, like small shallow temples, were set up, and some of the sculptured portraits were extremely good. The body was laid out in the home and mourned by the family: the family wore black and cut their hair short, giving their long locks to the dead. The laments might be sung by a choir and in one case the great Boeotian poet, Pindar, wrote a lament for an Athenian. The body in this period was sometimes cremated, sometimes simply buried. It was brought in procession to the family plot where the monument was set up. If there was a funeral feast, the pots were broken after use and left there. Afterwards relations and friends would often bring to the grave the tall white-lekythoi containing the perfume. (These vases were in so far a sham, as the perfume container itself was quite small in proportion to the whole vase.)

The area including the Cemeteries outside the Dipylon gate and up the road to the boundary of the Agora and a bit into the Agora itself was called Kerameikos, potters' quarter, for it was in this area that the potters had their workshops and sold their pots. This industry must have been of considerable size: for red-figure painted pottery alone, from about 530 to about 330 BC, some 1,100 potters and painters can be distinguished on stylistic grounds, and some 21,000 surviving pots have been attributed to them, but this must be a tiny fraction of what was actually made. The Panathenaic prize-amphorae alone, as we have seen, amounted to over 1,000 at each festival, which would mean that the total output of this one shape was over 50,000 between 530 and 330. The demand for pots for special occasions, also meant that many excellent artists were on hand to receive commissions. At a guess the total number of men making and painting red-figure pots at any one time might be about 150.

The prices that we know vary from half a drachma for the empty, second-hand Panathenaic amphorae in the auction-lists to three drachmai scratched on the bottom of a hydria with a not-very interesting picture of women (and this again may have been a second-hand price). Euphronios, one of the better painters of the late sixth century, who employed several other very good painters in his pottery shop in the early fifth century, dedicated a marble statue, about 480, to Athena 'as a tithe'. Presumably this was to mark an exceptionally good year or something of that kind: the statue would not cost less than 500 drachmai so that Euphronios must have made about 5,000 drachmai that year. If, for instance, he had been entrusted with the production of Panathenaic amphorae for a festival, that might perhaps have been the sort of occasion to justify dedicating a statue to Athena. The names that we have for potters and painters sometimes suggest slaves—Lydian, Brygan, Scythian; but the inference is not safe, as the noble young Kroisos with his foreign name shows, and names like Andokides, Euphronios, Douris, were also borne by well-known historical characters, and the painter Euthymides, who once wrote gaily on a pot, 'Better than any Euphronios', was the son of a sculptor.

The pictures of potteries suggest that the actual shops were small, perhaps employing five or six men. They also show that coarse pottery—storage pithoi and kitchen-ware—was produced in the same shops. The beautifully glazed Athenian lamps must also have been made in the vase-shops. One would expect also that the potteries produced the roof tiles, which were often beautifully decorated in vase technique with formal patterns. All this would raise an estimate of numbers of craftsmen by an amount which cannot be calculated.

Terracotta statuettes, of which quantities were needed for dedications to gods and offerings to the dead, were probably also sometimes made here: the same clay was used, some figurines were

25 Bronze foundry

26 Hephaisteion, showing Acropolis and east end of Agora
(on extreme left)

decorated with the same glaze paint as vases and used as vases or
mounted on vases. But one terracotta workshop was certainly
quite near the houses at the foot of the Areopagos (p. 28). The
actual moulds for the finest terracotta statuettes may have come
from the neighbouring bronze-workers, but this has not been
finally proved by the discovery of an identical figure in bronze
and clay. The larger terracotta statues, for instance the akroteria
which stood on the top and outside corners of pediments and were
often of terracotta instead of marble, must have been the work of
large-scale sculptors who otherwise worked in bronze or stone. We
have seen already the inside of a shop making metal vases; a red-
figure cup has a picture of a bronze-sculptor's shop with a bronze
statue partly assembled (25). And in the part of the Agora to the
south-west of the temple of Hephaistos, workshops and moulds for
bronze statues have been discovered. The street which ran through
this area south-west towards the Pnyx was found, when excavated,
to have so many bits of half-carved marble that it must have been
the quarter occupied by sculptors in marble. The two quarters on
either side of the temple of Hephaistos were so close that inter-
change of ideas in this group of related crafts must have been easy,

58

and this may in part account for the uniform swift movement of style in Attic art.

From soon after 430 BC the new temple of Hephaistos at Athens must have dominated these quarters and the Agora itself, as it does today (26–7). The bronze cult-statues of Hephaistos and Athena were made by Alkamenes between 421 and 415, and stood on a base which had a relief illustrating the birth of Erichthonios, one of the earlier mythical kings of Athens: Ge, the earth, holds the child up to Athena, symbolising the Athenian claim to belong to Attica, which had never been conquered by foreigners. Hephaistos was the smith-god and the fire-god (he wears a smith's cap and a workman's short chiton, and holds a hammer above an anvil), and is very relevant to this quarter; Athena was a general patron of the arts besides being the goddess of Athens. The sculpture on the outside of the temple, pediments, metopes and frieze, which shows the labours of Theseus and Herakles, is less obviously relevant: but both heroes were protected by Athena in their adventures. Theseus was an Athenian, and in the late sixth century he seems to have become the national hero of the Kleisthenic democracy; in 475 BC his bones were brought back from the island of Skyros, where he was said to have died, and were buried in a precinct in the south-west of the Agora, which had near it a set of dining rooms where feasts in his honour would be held, and which was decorated by the great painters Mikon and Polygnotoes. Herakles was an international Greek hero but was immensely popular in Athens, to judge by the enormous number of pictures of him on Attic vases, and he was the one hero who appeared on the east pediment of the

27   Interior of the Temple of Hephaistos

Parthenon watching the birth of Athena (see below, p. 142). He had a special connection with Marathon: in the picture of the battle painted for the Stoa Poikile in the Agora about 460, he appears with Theseus and Athena to encourage the Greeks, and in Euripides' *Heraclidae* it was Marathon where his sons and daughters took refuge from the pursuit of Eurystheus, King of Argos. At the end of Euripides' *Hercules*, Theseus brings him to Athens after he has murdered his wife and children in Thebes, and makes over to him his own shrines and rites. In some sense the friendship and the sharing of exploits symbolises a desired harmony between the old families and new democratic Athens.

Much of the Agora was taken up with shops, and every sort of thing could be bought there. The Athenians would not have appreciated the super-market. According to Xenophon, writing about 360, 'any servant you tell to go and buy something for you in the Agora, will have no difficulty: he will certainly know where to go and find such things. The reason is that each is in its appointed place.' The places were called after what was sold there; so a character in comedy said, 'I went round to the garlic and the onions and the frankincense and the perfume.'

We know a little about where some things were sold. Presumably the potters, bronze-workers and marble-workers used their work-shops as shops at any rate for special orders, but we do also know of 'the lamps' and 'the cooking pots', and a place where cooks can hire pots, and these are probably shops in the Agora. Simon the cobbler had his house, which was also his shop, in the south-west corner of the Agora close to the boundary stone. Free men who wanted jobs were on hire near the Hephaisteion; slaves who could be hired gathered near the shrine of the Dioskouroi on the slopes of the Acropolis.

Barbers, fishmongers and bankers all worked on the north side. Barber-shops were noted centres of gossip in Athens, as they have always been everywhere. The fishmongers were accused of charg-ing exorbitant prices and of wetting their fish unduly to make them overweight. In a commercial city like Athens with such a widespread system of overseas commerce, the bankers must have been important. We have already seen how extremely successful the slave Pasion was as a banker. Olive oil was sold over on the east side. Books were sold in the Orchestra: probably the name, which means dancing-floor, had lingered on from the location of the theatre in the Agora, where comedy was performed until it was transferred to the theatre of Dionysos on the south slope of the Acropolis. The Orchestra was probably in the centre of the Agora.

The word 'shop' is somewhat misleading. Probably there were five different sorts of erections where things could be sold, and these should be distinguished. First there were the houses with workshops attached, like the house of Simon the cobbler, and the workshops of the sculptors and potters: these must have been permanent buildings. Secondly, in one case we hear of a portico (stoa) in which things were sold: this was the stoa where groats were sold, and it was probably on the road between the Agora and the Dipylon gate. Thirdly, there were rings (kykloi); they were presumably round platforms on which salesmen could display their wares. They were used for meat, fish, textiles, pots, and also for displaying slaves on sale. Fourthly, there were tables, which were certainly used by the bankers, but also by others. Lastly, there were booths.

Except for the permanent workshops the whole aspect of the Agora must have been much more like a fair or a market held in an open market-place than a modern shopping centre. The plane trees planted by Kimon must have given welcome shade. But in spite of this informal aspect there was considerable control of commercial activity. Ten controllers of measures (metronomoi) were chosen by lot every year, and sets of standard weights and measures (28) have been found, and a gauge for standardising tiles: one set was kept in the round-building (tholos) on the west side of the Agora. Ten grain-guardians (sitophylakes) fixed the price of grain, and regulated in accordance with this the price both of milled corn and bakery products. Ten market officials (agoranomoi) saw that the produce sold was genuine and unadulterated. The Peiraeus had its own metronomoi, sitophylakes and agoranomoi to deal with the mass of imported corn. Ten town officials (astynomoi) had a curious mixture of duties: besides preventing dustmen depositing rubbish

28 Measures

29   Foot-race from Panathenaic amphora

within ten stades of the walls, and preventing housebuilders either blocking up roads or building out balconies or having gutters which poured water down on to the road or allowing windows to open on to the road, they also controlled the price of flute-girls and harpists and saw that they were not hired for more than two drachmai an evening.

There were occasions when the central area of the Agora was cleared, or partially cleared. When comedies were still performed in the Agora, stands for spectators were erected round the dancing-floor or orchestra. The Panathenaic Way ran diagonally across the Agora, and when every fourth year the great procession was held, crowds assembled to see it, and it has been suggested that the cuttings along the Panathenaic Way on the north-east side were meant to take stands. Also a good deal of space must have been needed for the race of men in armour held in the Agora at the Panathenaic Festival. They raced in chariots and at a certain moment jumped from their chariots and ran to a point, then had to run back and jump on the moving chariot again. Probably all the athletic contests of the Panathenaic games (29) took place in the Agora until the stadium was built outside the city walls in the late fourth century.

Apart from all this, the Athenian democracy from the time of Kleisthenes needed space for the curious practice of ostracism, a method of getting rid, for ten years, of a citizen who seemed undesirably powerful. Each year the Assembly was asked whether an ostracism should be held. If they voted for this, a day was fixed and the centre of the Agora was enclosed by a fence with ten doors, one for each of the Kleisthenic Tribes (phylai). On the day, everyone who wanted to vote wrote the name of the man he wished to be rid of on a bit of pot (ostrakon)—or accepted from some political agent a sherd with a name already written on it—entered the enclosure by the entrance for his tribe and gave up his ostrakon to an official. He then had to stay in the enclosure until all the votes were counted. If they totalled more than 6,000, then the man who got the most votes was exiled for ten years. Perikles was greatly aided in his democratic programme by the ostracism of two leading conservative politicians, Kimon, son of Miltiades (the victor of Marathon), about 460, and Thucydides, son of Melesias, about 443. Ostracism was not the equivalent of a general election, but had something of the same effect.

With the clearing of the Agora for ostracism we pass from the Agora as a commercial centre to the Agora as a civic centre. Before the end of the fifth century the Agora had a number of imposing public buildings of which a few must be mentioned. The three stoai or porticos were good places for meeting friends and talking, but had other functions too, some of them political. The earliest was the Stoa of the Herms on the north side, which was built round and over the three stone Herms (pillars with heads of Hermes on the top and genitals half-way down), commemorating Kimon's victory over the Persians in 475. These were among the Herms mutilated on the famous night in 415. Young cavalrymen (who came from the second Athenian property class) were often to be found there, and this is perhaps why Sokrates came here; these were the young men who liked discussing with him. It is also probable that this stoa was used as a rehearsal place for boys' choruses, because boys' choruses are sometimes illustrated in front of a pillared building with a herm.

Just to the east of the Stoa of the Herms was the Stoa Poikile, the 'painted stoa', so-called because of its pictures. It was built about 460 by Kimon's brother-in-law Peisianax, and the walls were decorated with pictures on panels by the famous painters Polygnotos, Mikon and Panainos (p. 127). It was not only a picture-gallery: there was room enough for a trial with a jury of 500 men, and official arbitrations were also held there. Just after our period Zenon used to lecture there and so the Stoics got their name.

On the other side of the Stoa of the Herms, at the north end of the west side of the Agora, was a fine later fifth-century building with wings, known both as the Royal Stoa and the Stoa of Zeus. It did not get its pictures until the mid-fourth century when Euphranor painted three great pictures (p. 179). Zeus was called here Eleutherios, Zeus of Freedom, celebrating the freedom of Athens from Persian domination; his statue stood on a round base in front of the building. The other name, Royal (which almost certainly goes back to an earlier building before the new stoa), refers to its use as the office of the Archon Basileus or King Archon, who was in charge of many aspects of religion. He (and his two assessors) let out the sacred lands on ten-year leases, he made arrangements for the older sacrifices and festivals, like the Eleusinian Mysteries and the winter festival of Dionysos (the Lenaia) with its procession and contest of comedies and tragedies, and for all torch-races. He was also in charge of all lawsuits concerned with impiety (like the suit against Sokrates), and with disputes about priesthoods, and with all murder cases, which were tried in different courts according to the nature of the crime. Murder with forethought was tried by the Council of the Areopagos and it sometimes sat in the Royal Stoa, in a part roped off to give it privacy. When the constitution was revised at the end of the Peloponnesian War, the laws were inscribed on marble slabs set up in the stoa.

Next to the Stoa of Zeus on the west side was the temple of Apollo Patroos with a cult-statue by Euphranor (p. 181). This temple replaced a much earlier temple. The 'paternal' Apollo is closely connected with the phratriai (brotherhoods) in which Athenian families were originally organised. This is an older organisation than the Kleisthenic organisation by demes, and the Athenian boy had to be accepted by his phratria at an early age and was then registered in the temple of Apollo Patroos.

The rest of the west side of the Agora was occupied by a complex of buildings, the temple of the Mother of the Gods, the Council House and the Round-Building (tholos). Quite why the Mother of the Gods, identified both with Rhea, the mother of Zeus, and with the Asiatic nature-goddess Kybele, should have her shrine in this very official quarter is not clear. But as she was there, her temple was used as a store-house for public records, which were looked after by a state slave (demosios).

The Council House was the headquarters of the Kleisthenic Council (Boule) of 500. They were elected by lot, 50 from each tribe, and served for a year. Each set of tribal members served in turn as a committee (prytaneis) for 36 or 35 days, and for that period took their meals in the Tholos, with one-third constantly on duty. They convened the Council every day except holidays and arranged its order of business; and they convened the Assembly on four days in each 36-day period and arranged its business. They also checked the qualifications of various officials and how they used their funds, and they scrutinised the councillors and archons of the next year. They supervised the building of triremes (warships), the docks and all public buildings. Under the Council also were the poletai (sellers), who let out the silver mines and all other state contracts, and sold the property of the condemned (like those who profaned the Mysteries and mutilated the Herms in 415). The Council performed many other tasks such as electing state auditors from their own number, scrutinising the horses of the cavalry, scrutinising cripples, who, if they could pass a means test, were entitled to a pension, and supervising the election of the ten strategoi (generals), who were nominally military and naval commanders, but actually, as one sees from the example of Perikles, something more like a modern cabinet. Their offices may have been a building just south-west of the Tholos.

Just beyond Simon the cobbler's house, outside the Agora there is another group of offices which presumably housed some of the numerous officials, and more offices probably existed on the south side, including perhaps the offices called after the Thesmothetai, the six junior archons. They were legal officials who fixed the calendar for all sorts of cases, and were responsible for introducing into assembly certain treason cases, and for certain private suits connected with citizenship, trade, mines and slaves. They also ratified treaties. The senior archons apparently only moved into these offices in Solon's time. Before that the Eponymous Archon, so called because he gave his name to the year, had his office in the Prytaneion, which was under the north-east end of the Acropolis. This had the sacred fire always burning, of which colonists took a portion when they set out from Athens. And here

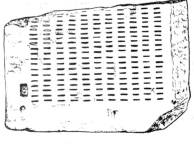

30 Allotment machine

public benefactors, including victors in the Panhellenic games (Olympic, Pythian, Nemean and Isthmian), were entertained. It also served as a law-court for certain kinds of cases. It is not quite clear how many of the functions of the Prytaneion were transferred to the Tholos when it was built.

The Eponymous Archon, early in his year of office, made the arrangements for the necessary numbers of rich men to finance the dramatic and choral productions at the festivals of Dionysos (the City Dionysia) and Apollo (the Thargelia). Dramatic productions will occupy us later. These were comparatively new religious celebrations, and therefore fell to him instead of to the King Archon. He was particularly concerned with lawsuits about inheritances, and about the affairs of heiresses and orphans and widows.

The third senior archon (the Polemarch) lost his military functions when the ten strategoi were instituted. His original seat was probably in Kynosarges, where the gymnasium was used for military training. He kept charge of sacrifices to Enyalios (the war-god) and of funeral offerings to those who were killed in war, and he arranged funeral games. He was also concerned with the legal affairs of resident aliens.

The account of city life so far given has referred both to law-courts and to different kinds of litigation. Litigation was so varied and frequent in Athens that there were certainly more law-courts than those that have been mentioned. In the Agora a series of large walled courtyards on the east side were law-courts, and there were probably more on the south-west. What we know for certain from literary sources is that there were a number of courts, that the Athenians believed in large juries, and that elaborate precautions were taken to avoid corruption.

In the oldest court, the Heliaia, juries were 1,001 and more (the odd number prevented the votes being equal), and in many other courts 501. Every citizen over the age of 30 had the right to sit on a jury, and to judge from Aristophanes' *Wasps*, the older men thoroughly enjoyed this, and the small payment, a third of a skilled workman's wages, was well worth having. The system was a fundamental part of Athenian democracy as a means by which poorer men could both control the activities of richer men and see that their own equals were justly treated.

Excavation has brought to view a number of objects which throw light on the procedure. A man who wanted to be a juryman had to appear at the place allotted to his phyle, and then with his fellow-tribesmen he drew lots for a ticket, which gave the letter of the court in which he was to serve. On the morning of a day he wanted to serve, he went back and put his ticket in a box labelled with the court letter. Then a complicated machine (*30*) ensured that a random selection of jurors should be allotted to each court that was going to sit on that day; the rest were dismissed. The jurors were given a bronze ball with the letter of the court so that they could make their way there, and their tickets were also taken to the court so that they could ultimately reclaim them there and be paid (this check was to prevent a juror helping a friend who was on trial by going to sit in the court which tried his friend instead of the one allotted to him). Only when the jury was in court were lots drawn for the presiding magistrate, and after that one juror was drawn to work the water-clock and four to count the votes.

The plaintiff and the defendant spoke for themselves, but they usually got their speeches written by a professional speech-writer. What we call today 'the Greek Orators' are largely the speeches written by speech-writers like Lysias or Demosthenes for particular cases and subsequently polished up for publication as teaching-material for their pupils. The speeches were limited in time according to the size of the penalty involved and were timed by the water-clock (*31*), which was stopped during the reading of documents or calling of testimony. After the speeches the judges are given two bronze votes, one with a hollow knob and one with a solid knob, the hollow one for the plaintiff and

31 Water-clock

the solid one for the defendant. They are careful not to show the parties which vote they put into the valid urn and which into the urn for discards. The votes are turned out and counted by the jurors allotted to this task, and the man with the most valid votes wins his suit.

Besides the suits tried in the various courts a number of suits went to arbitration. Cases involving no more than ten drachmai went to 40 judges who circulated through the demes. Cases involving more went to arbitrators over 60 years of age: only absence from the country or holding another office excused from this service.

It is extraordinary how much public service the male Athenian might do. He had two years military training (ephebe service). From the age of 20 to the age of 60 he was liable for military or naval service in the cavalry, heavy-infantry, light-armed troops or navy, according to his property qualifications. An estimate for the time of the Peloponnesian War gives 1,200 cavalry, 2,500 infantry and 2,000 naval ratings on the pay-roll in one year. After the age of 60 he could be called on to serve as arbitrator. The lists of ephebes

32 Pnyx with Acropolis in the background

and the call-up notices for military service were posted by the statues of the Eponymous Heroes of the phylai, which stood on a long base in the Agora opposite the Council House. There, too, were notices of lawsuits waiting to be tried and notices of laws to be proposed to the Assembly.

The Athenian also took part in the Assembly, which had 40 ordinary meetings a year, and public slaves rounded them up from the Agora on to the Pnyx for these meetings with the aid of a ruddled rope: anyone found afterwards with red on his clothes was fined. As we have seen, 6,000 was the quorum when the Assembly met in the Agora for ostracism, and presumably the important debates, like the decision in 415, to send an expedition to conquer Sicily, attracted that sort of number. The pay for attending the Assembly rose to half a drachma in the early fourth century.

The meeting of the Assembly which decided to send the expedition to Sicily was perhaps a routine meeting. A commission had been sent to Sicily and returned with a favourable report, and the Athenians decided to send 60 ships with their strategoi, Nikias,

Alkibiades and Lamachos. Five days later, a special assembly was held. Nikias spoke against the expedition and asked the presiding committee of the Council to put the matter to the vote again. Most of the speakers were in favour of the expedition, and Alkibiades made a passionate speech against Nikias. After more speeches in favour of the expedition, including speeches from pro-Athenian Sicilians, Nikias stressed the need for a very large expeditionary force. After still more speeches in favour of the expedition, Nikias was asked what forces he needed. He said that he would consult his colleagues on details, but he would need at least 100 triremes and 5,000 heavy-armed infantry with the rest of the armament in proportion. The Athenians promptly voted that the strategoi should have full powers to do what they thought best.

The account from the historian Thucydides gives the impression of a long and lively debate, and the Pnyx (32) must have presented a remarkable spectacle with its slopes crowded with some 6,000 Athenians. At the bottom was the platform which the speakers mounted one by one to address the audience. The presiding Committee of Council probably sat on either side of the platform facing the audience. A Herald introduced the speakers. Order was kept by the Archers, who formed the Athenian police-force. Voting was by show of hands.

More of the flavour comes out in Aristophanes' satyric account of the Assembly at the beginning of the *Acharnians* in 425: the fury of the old countryman who has arrived early in the Pnyx for a regular Assembly, hoping to discuss peace in the Peloponnesian War, to find no one there. 'They are all talking in the Agora and running away from the ruddled rope.' Then the presiding Committee arrives and jostles for seats. The Herald asks for a speaker and a man proposes himself as an envoy to Sparta. The Herald calls on the Archers to deal with him. Then there is an Athenian delegation bringing a special emissary from Persia, who is finally invited to dinner in the Prytaneion by the presiding Committee. Then the Herald summons an envoy from Thrace who suggests that a Thracian king will send the Athenians mercenaries and brings in some specimens. The old countryman is so furious that he says he can feel a drop of rain, and that is a portent from Zeus. The Herald accepts the portent as a reason for dissolving the Assembly.

The Athenian could also, as we have seen, do jury service, and the estimate already quoted for military service gives 6,000 jury-men. This is presumably a maximum, but juries of 501 were comparatively common and ten courts might be sitting at any one time.

When we look at officials, we find only a few elected officials and nearly all of them in the armed forces: ten strategoi, two cavalry commanders, ten infantry and ten cavalry colonels, ten cavalry recruiting officers, eleven officers to look after the ephebes, two physical-training instructors for the ephebes, and an unknown number of instructors in military-training. Outside these we only hear of the treasurer of the military funds, the treasurer of the funds used for spectacles, and the supervisor of fountains.

The vast majority of offices were filled by lot, and the list which Aristotle gives in the *Constitution of Athens* is worth quoting.

500 Councillors, who were allowed to serve again once
 10 Treasurers of Athena
 10 Poletai (sellers)
 10 Receivers
 10 Auditors
 10 Assistants to the auditors
 10 Examiners (to examine the conduct of officials at the end of their year of office)
 20 Assessors to the examiners
 10 Commissioners for the maintenance of sacred places
 10 Astynomoi
 10 Agoranomoi
 10 Metronomoi
 35 Sitophylakes
 10 Inspectors of cargoes
 11 Police officers (who dealt with thefts and similar crimes, and are in charge of the prison)
  5 Magistrates (to decide cases which have to be decided within a month)
 40 Deme judges
  5 Commissioners of roads
  3 Clerks
 20 Hieropoioi (in charge of sacrifices)
  1 Archon for Salamis
  1 Demarchon for the Peiraeus

    9 Archons
   10 Officials of the games (in charge of the Panathenaic Festival
      and Mysteries, in office for four years)
  100 Guards of the dockyards and of the Acropolis
1,130 Deme officials and other civil officials who served outside the
      city

2,000

In all this list the councillors were the only officers who were allowed to serve in the same office again and they could serve twice. There is a very clear distinction between the elected officers, chiefly military, where experience was believed to matter and there was no ban on re-election, and the offices held by lot where the object seems to have been to have the office held by the maximum number of people. How did these officers get sufficient knowledge? Sometimes presumably there was an efficient slave as a permanent clerk, although we do not hear much of this type of permanent civil service. Every kind of transaction was recorded so that a new officer could look at the precedents. In a great many cases the boards had one officer from each phyle and presumably the predecessor in the phyle might be known and could be very helpful to the new officer. Certainly, as we have seen, there were plenty of checks to prevent corruption—audits, appeals to law-courts, and the like. But much must have depended on general political experience, listening to the debates in the Assembly, serving on juries, serving on council, having held other offices, and on the shrewdness that the man had developed in his own career.

If the first surprise is that a system of civil government entirely based on amateurs could work, as it evidently did, the second surprise is that the amateurs found time enough to work it, since something like eight per cent of the adult male citizens were in office every year. The pay, as far as we know it, was minimal and can never have been more than a partial compensation for giving this time to the state. The councillors certainly had a full-time job during the month when their section formed the committee, but the full council met every day except for holidays. It would be extremely interesting to know how much time had to be spent on the other offices, and probably they varied greatly. Presumably most of them were held by men living in Athens, except for the deme judgeships and the deme offices and the various market offices expressly assigned to the Peiraeus, which would be held by locals. But when every allowance is made the classical Athenian must be credited with a good deal of public spirit and a considerable knowledge of public affairs, both in general and in detail. He needed (in the words of Perikles) to have the power of adapting himself to the most varied forms of action with versatility and grace.

4

Religion and festivals

Science, philosophy, technology and psychology have taken over many areas of human experience which formerly belonged to religion. It would be truer perhaps to say that in the minds of some people they have taken over these spheres, while for some the conquest is much less complete, and most people are inconsistent somewhere. But most people explain and try to control physical events like droughts and floods by physical means; they do not explain them as divine interference or try to control them by ritual. Most people, if they want to become technologists, pay fees to a technological school; a classical Greek would have apprenticed himself to a craftsman, but would also have prayed for the help of Hephaistos or Athena and would have felt bound to make them an offering if successful. Most people pay a doctor for curing them (unless they get their cure free fom the Health Service), but a Greek would also make a dedication to Asklepios as the god of healing. If someone is outstanding or abnormal, we explain his behaviour by psychology, whereas a Greek would commonly suppose that he had been helped or harmed by a god.

The scientific revolution had started in Greece in the sixth century and made considerable progress through the classical period, giving rise to the same sort of conflicts that Darwin and Freud have produced in modern times. We shall see some instances later in considering Greek poetry and art. But for the Greeks the scientific approach was extremely new and their scientists had barely begun to develop technique and apparatus; it was also the preserve of a very small number of people, while the rest remained content with the religious approach. Plutarch's *Life of Pericles* has a nice illustration of the situation. In about 445 a ram was found with only one horn growing from the middle of its forehead. It was a portent which needed explaining. The seer Lampon said that it was an omen for the future: now there were two strong men in Athenian politics, the conservative Thucydides, son of Melesias, and the radical Perikles; soon there would only be one. The philosopher-scientist Anaxagoras split the ram's head open and showed that the single horn was due to a malformation of the skull. Two years later Thucydides, son of Melesias, was ostracized, and everybody knew that Lampon was right.

The two areas in which we come nearest to Greek religion are first our recourse to religion in the natural crises of human life—birth, adolescence, marriage, death—and secondly some highly irrational and unscientific behaviour in everyday life—the oath when something strikes us unexpectedly, superstitions about black cats and spiders, the feeling that a dark wood is sinister, our traditional ceremonies and traditional dress. For the classical Greek, both areas were part of a generally religious approach to life; for us they are outlying survivals of a religious approach after we have for the most part put science in the centre.

In the religion of classical Athens, many layers of thought about the gods coexist, and it may be useful to try and mention some of these distinctions first as a guide to understanding the actual practices. For instance, the little girls in the temple of Artemis at Brauron who were called Bears (p. 21) must be a survival of a stage when Artemis herself was a big bear. This must almost have been before the Greeks came to Greece, since bears are unknown in classical Greece. In Mycenaean times gods evidently appeared to men as birds, but they themselves had human form; therefore, although Athena may have originally been an owl, this must have been before Mycenaean times. But the owl remains Athena's favourite bird, and as such appears on Athenian coins and sometimes on vases (*33*). More generally, birds were thought to predict the future, and whereas in classical times most people did not believe any more that the gods appeared as birds, they did believe that the behaviour of birds could show them what was going to happen

33   An owl:
the bird of Athena

75

in the future: the gods knew the future and skilful men could interpret the flight of birds whom the gods sent to give us this knowledge.

There were many other ways of foretelling the future—the constitution of a sacrificial victim's liver, signs from heaven like thunder and lightning, sooth-sayers, oracles. It is, of course, natural to believe that an omnipotent god is also omniscient. But it is a curious difference between Greek and Christian thought that the Greek had also no doubt that he could tap this knowledge. He might and often did mistrust the human beings who interpreted the divine signs for him, but he did not doubt that they were there to be interpreted if the right interpretation could be found. So whereas we feel somewhat ashamed if we resort to fortune-tellers or astrologers, the Greek would be unlikely to undertake any important public or private enterprise without consulting an oracle or taking the omens.

When the oracles got the answer wrong, their priests were quite clever in inventing excuses. The Athenians naturally consulted the oracle of Zeus at Dodona in western Greece before undertaking the Sicilian expedition. The question was inscribed on a lead-tablet in the form: 'Is it better for the Athenians to send an expedition to Sicily?' The oracle answered in the affirmative. When the expedition proved disastrous, the priests said that there was a small hill near Athens which was called Sicily, and Zeus meant them to go there. Sometimes elaborate precautions were taken to get an unbiased answer. In 352 the Athenians wanted to know whether to build a stoa on some land or whether to leave it as a sacred meadow. Each alternative was written on a tin tablet and wrapped up. The wrapped tablets were put in a jar. Then one was drawn out and put in a silver jar, and the other into a golden jar. Then the Athenians sent a commission of three men to the oracle of Apollo at Delphi to ask whether they should follow the tablet in the golden jar or the tablet in the silver jar. Thus the god had to choose between two unknown alternatives.

More important than tapping the gods' knowledge was directing the gods' power. The Greeks thought of their gods as human, and therefore when they wanted to control the workings of nature, they took for their model some human process. The major problem was the renewal of life in the spring: there must be new crops, new olives, new grapes, new lambs, new kids, new calves and new children. The earth mother must give birth to all this, and the model is human procreation. So a great deal of ritual was designed for this purpose, and we shall see this in the festivals, particularly of Demeter, Athena and Dionysos.

Often ritual gave rise to, or was accompanied by, myth. In the early stages the song was sung while the ritual was being performed, explaining the ritual in human terms. For instance, it seems almost certain that the story of Theseus abandoning Ariadne asleep on Naxos so that she was then found by Dionysos was a myth about the sleep of the earth in winter and her reawakening in spring, and it could be sung to accompany a ritual of marriage between the goddess and the god who was to give her new fertility. Other myths tell of the past exploits of the gods to make them powerful for new exploits. But once a myth has been told, it takes on a life of its own as a story: the ritual and the cult may be forgotten by later poets and artists who reinterpret the story to suit their own day (we shall consider some instances in the next chapter).

When the gods were thought of as human, two further ideas naturally came in. They have human pleasures and therefore may be pleased by what pleases us: they can share our meal when we sacrifice to them, they will enjoy beautiful works of art, they will enjoy good poetry (whether it is about them themselves or not), and they will enjoy seeing men dancing, boxing or racing. In fact, the idea of the festival is born. To give these human gods an offering is the natural way to secure their favour. It does not matter what sort of gods they are: whether it is an earth-goddess like Demeter, or a patron of a craft like Hephaistos, or a personification of wild nature like Pan, or the personification of a curiously shaped place like the tunnel god Serangos, or the presumed inhabitant of a rediscovered beehive tomb like the Hero near Acharnai, they are all powerful for good or evil and can be made kindly by sacrifice or offerings.

If the gods are human and powerful, then another idea comes in and had come in by the eighth century. If often appears that the morally good come to disaster and the morally bad flourish. It would be nice if these human and powerful gods ruled the world so that the virtuous were rewarded and the guilty were punished. A lot of religious thought has gone into this problem at all times and in all countries, and the Greeks were no exception. Some

34–5   Chous

of their solutions we shall notice in the chapter on poetry and art.

Finally, the festival comes to be more a holiday than a Holy Day. Perikles, in the speech which he delivered to commemorate those who had fallen in the first year of the Peloponnesian War, drew a picture of fifth-century Athens and the fifth-century Athenian as he saw them. Among the other advantages of Athens, he noted 'the contests and sacrifices throughout the year, which provide us with more relaxation from work than exists in any other city'. The religious reason for a festival is forgotten: it is simply a holiday.

In a brief chapter it is impossible to do more than pick out certain topics for illustration, some of the offerings made, some of the great festivals. Religion entered into private life all the time. For those in the country, Pan and the Nymphs of the springs were very present deities. Olive crops, vintage, and corn harvest would only go right if offerings were made to Athena, Dionysos and Demeter. Most houses had a Herm before the door and an altar of Zeus and Apollo in the courtyard; the hearth was protected by Hestia, the hearth goddess. They all needed their offerings. The introduction of children into the brotherhoods (phratriai) involved a sacrifice to Zeus and Athena, as gods of the phratria at a festival called the Apatouria. The children also, at the age of three, took part in a Dionysos festival called Anthesteria, which will concern us later: the children were wreathed with flowers and received as presents tiny jugs, which were models of the wine jugs used by their elders on the same day (34-5). At the age of 18 the boy had his long hair cut at the same phratria festival at which he had been introduced as a child. He then became an ephebe, and was accepted in his deme: some of the ephebes' first year of training was spent in visiting and making offerings at holy places and taking part in religious processions. Marriage naturally involved many religious practices: the bride offered her hair to Artemis. The goodwill of Zeus and Hera, as guardians of marriage, had to be secured. Special water for the bride-bath was brought from a sacred spring. After the marriage the bridegroom made an offering at the next Apatouria because his wife was a new member of the phratria.

Sacrificial offerings made to the gods ranged from a piece of frankincense or a cake to animals singly or in number. Dedications might be a rough terracotta statuette or a beautifully painted vase or a costly statue. Naturally an enormous number of dedications were made on the Acropolis of Athens and the vast majority of them were dedicated to Athena. About 400 inscribed pieces of marble —bases for marble or bronze statues, pillars with reliefs, supports for bronze bowls, altars, marble basins—have survived and can be dated from the mid-sixth to the mid-fifth century.

A few specimens will give some idea of the range of dedicators. Kallimachos was the polemarch in the year of the battle of Marathon. Someone from his deme dedicated to Athena on the Acropolis a marble female flying figure, described in the inscription as 'messenger of the immortals who hold the broad heaven', probably, therefore, Iris as the messenger of the gods. The inscription goes on that Kallimachos as polemarch made the contest between Persians and Greeks and died in the grove of Marathon defending the sons of Athens from slavery. 'Made the contest' is a curious phrase, the phrase used for an official who presided over the games. So this great match between East and West brought death to Kallimachos and freedom to the Greeks. Iris was perhaps chosen as the news had to be brought from Marathon to Athens.

A marble figure of a boy has been connected with an inscribed column naming Kallias, son of Didymias, as victor in a boys' contest, probably at the Panathenaic festival in 482. He was victorious at Olympia in 472 and dedicated another statue there, made by the Athenian sculptor Mikon, who was also a great painter. Later still about 450 Kallias made another dedication on the Acropolis of a bronze statue; on the base he recorded, in addition to these two victories, ten at the Pythian games, five at the Isthmian, and four at the Nemean games. He was a successful athlete at all the great Greek festivals: presumably he was given free meals in the Prytaneion by the Athenians. He showed his gratitude by dedicating his statue to Athena.

A victory in one of the great games was a cause of national rejoicing, and Pindar or some other great lyric poet of the day was engaged to write an ode in praise of the athlete, describing his victory, tracing his pedigree if his ancestors were famous, telling a story of heroic myth which was more or less applicable, and drawing a serious moral about human life. The ode was sung and danced by a choir, sometimes at a feast immediately following the victory, sometimes when the victor had returned home, and it might, if it proved popular, pass into the repertory of symposion songs. Not only the athletic victors in the Panathenaia dedicated their statues to Athena: the musical victors did the same—an inscription survives from the base of a bronze statue of a kitharoidos, a singer who accompanied himself on the big concert lyre (p. 49).

Many of the dedications are made by officials or by men whom we know otherwise as officials—the captain of a trireme (who was also the father of a tragic poet), three cavalry commanders (who dedicated a bronze group of a man leading a horse), the committee of the Boule in 408–407 BC, who were judged the most successful committee of their year. A man who later became a treasurer of Athena set up a bronze statue as the 'first-fruits' of his wealth in fulfilment of a vow, and prays Athena in gratitude to preserve his wealth.

We have already noticed that the potter and vase-painter Euphronios dedicated a statue to Athena. One of his best painters was Onesimos, and he also dedicated a statue as 'first-fruits'; but we also have pieces of no less than seven marble basins dedicated by him as 'first-fruits'. It is not quite clear whether these were all one dedication; probably they were, as the writing seems to date them all together some 15 years later than the statue. Onesimos must have had some specially profitable commission on two occasions. Besides potters, we have dedications by a fuller, a tanner, a builder, a shipbuilder, a clerk and a washerwoman. Any sort of success in Athens had to be celebrated by a gift to Athena.

In all these offerings the essential idea is given by an early inscription: 'Telesinos dedicates this statue to you, rejoicing in which grant him to dedicate another.' This is a simple commercial transaction, like the modern offertory. But the great festivals of Demeter, Athena, and Dionysos had as their foundation a very much older conception of deity: the possibility of ensuring by ritual that life was renewed in the spring. The idea is preserved most clearly in the Eleusinian Mysteries, in so far as the splendour with which they were celebrated is not so much the splendour of a holiday as the splendour of self-dedication. The myth of this ritual preserves very clearly the original intention. Demeter was herself already an earth-goddess in Mycenaean times. Her daughter, Persephone (or very often simply Kore, the girl), was gathering flowers. When she picked a narcissus, the earth opened and Plouton, the god of the underworld, came up in his chariot and carried her off. Demeter came to Eleusis searching for her daughter. They received her kindly and she told them to build her a temple. Then she shut herself up, and famine raged in the land. Finally Zeus forced Plouton to send Persephone back, but Plouton gave her first a pomegranate to eat. This ensured that she would have to spend a third of the year with Plouton in the underworld—the winter when the corn is not above ground. The essential idea is the agony of winter and the joy of returning new vegetation in the spring. And with the return of Persephone, Demeter sent out the Eleusinian prince, Triptolemos, to teach the world agriculture. But there is in the Mysteries another idea besides the essential agricultural idea: somehow there is a parallel between human life and the life of the seed; although the Mysteries cannot guarantee that the dead rise again, they can ensure that he has a life of bliss in the underworld, instead of the shadowy existence in which the Greeks normally believed. The temple at Eleusis already existed in Mycenaean times, and was repeatedly rebuilt and expanded. In the time of Perikles the shrine was a large square building (about 150 by 150 feet) with tiers of eight steps round the walls and an inner central shrine, which was lit by a lantern. Here the final rites took place after long preparations.

36   Initiation of Herakles and the Dioskouroi

The Lesser Mysteries were held in February on the banks of the River Ilissos, east of Athens, where a new temple was built to Demeter about 450. The rite was traditionally founded for the initiation of Herakles, because he was a foreigner. A fourth-century vase in the British Museum (*36*) shows him being presented to Demeter, Persephone and Triptolemos by an official of the cult, at the same time as another official presents the Dioskouroi, Kastor and Polydeukes, who could also be regarded as foreigners from Sparta. Thus these great benefactors of mankind were given an Athenian status. The columns behind stand for the temple or its gatehouse. This tells us nothing about the actual rites, which included purification and were regarded as a preparation for the Greater Mysteries. The time presumably coincided with Persephone's return from the underworld.

The Greater Mysteries were held in September, not more than a month before Persephone went down to Hades. This was an international festival, and initiates might come from all over the world. The date was, therefore, advertised by heralds sent by the two aristocratic families connected with this rite; they proclaimed a holy truce of 55 days and asked the Greek cities to send theoroi (observers). When they had arrived, the whole programme took seven days. On the day before, the sacred objects were brought in procession from Eleusis to Athens. What they were is unknown, but the priestesses carried them in round boxes (kistai) on their heads. They were met by the ephebes and escorted to the Eleusinion, the shrine of Demeter and Persephone, on the slopes of the Acropolis, just above the east end of the Agora.

On the first day of the Mysteries proper, a proclamation was made at the Stoa Poikile about the eligibility of the participants, and presumably instructions were given as to what was to be done. On the second day all the Mystics went down to the sea and washed both themselves and the little pigs, which they each sacrificed to the goddesses. On the third day the King Archon (as the traditional guardian of religion) offered a great sacrifice to the goddesses at the Eleusinion. The fourth day was a day of preparation for late-comers.

The great procession set forth on the 14-mile journey to Eleusis on the fifth day. It went out from the Dipylon gate. The statue of Iakchos (a personification of the shouts of the Mystics, just as the marriage-god Hymenaios is a personification of the marriage song) led the way on a carriage, then the priests and the priestesses with their kistai, then the state officials, the foreign observers, and lastly the Mystics. After the long march through the modern Daphni, as they wound over the bridge of the river before Eleusis, men with covered heads hurled abuse at them; this was a common and very old method of frightening away evil spirits. The procession finally arrived by torchlight, and the rest of the night was spent in singing and dancing in honour of the Eleusinian goddesses.

After that we know very little because the secrets were well preserved. Certainly they fasted; certainly they drank the kykeion, a mixture of meal and water, said to have been made and drunk by the goddess herself when she first came to Eleusis; certainly the King Archon made a sacrifice, and the ephebes took part in it by offering an ox and a libation bowl. So far all was public. Beyond that there were two stages: one for all the Mystics and one for the higher grade, the Epoptai, whose name 'viewers' implies that they saw something. It is possible that there was some sort of pageant of the abduction of Persephone, the wanderings of Demeter, and the reunion of mother and daughter. Certainly the sacred objects were shown, some to the Mystics and more to the Epoptai.

This all took the sixth and seventh days. On the eighth day libations were poured to the dead in special vessels, and a feast was held. On the ninth day they returned to their homes. The essential part of the rite is wrapped in secrecy. Somehow it gave those who went through it a new level of experience, as well as hope for a better life after death. For this the Mysteries were known over the whole Greek world, and it is easy to understand how shocking the Athenians found it that Alkibiades and his friends could parody the Mysteries in a private house.

It is surprising that the armed virgin goddess Athena should also be regarded as potent in the renewal of life in the spring but the evidence is clear, and it may be fair to say that the idea of the virgin-warrior is a later (though still probably Mycenaean) addition to an earlier fertility goddess. According to Pausanias, two girls, who lived on the Acropolis, were given by the priestess of Athena 'secret things' in kistai, which they took into an underground passage under the Acropolis and left there, bringing back other 'secret things' that they found there. When they came up, they were released from service, and other girls were brought to the Acropolis to take their place. This is explained as a burying of fertility symbols in June to make the earth fertile just before the harvest.

The girls were called Arrhephoroi (bearers of secret things). But there were two more of them, who were concerned with the making of the robe (peplos) for the most splendid festival of Athena, the Great Panathenaia. Thus this festival (which was founded in the early sixth century) was linked to the old fertility rite. These two girls with Athena's priestesses and others started the making of the peplos at a festival called Chalkeia (smithies) in October. The festival was especially celebrated by craftsmen, whose patron Athena was, but the offerings which they gave her were winnowing-fans—agriculture again. Then in May, well before the harvest, the wooden statue of the goddess had its robe removed and was taken to the sea in procession, escorted by the ephebes, was washed and brought back in a torchlight procession when it had been given a new robe. This is a bath of purification before the harvest, closely analogous to the bathing of the bride before her wedding. This is an old festival, which went on even when Athena was given a much more splendid robe at the Panathenaia.

The Panathenaia took place in July. Every four years the Great

Panathenaia was celebrated, and the peplos was offered to Athena. In the intervening years the Little Panathenaia was celebrated at the same date: it consisted of a night festival of dancing and singing (pannychis), a procession, a contest of 'circular choruses', and war-dances. Here no peplos was brought; this was simply a harvest festival for Athena. 'Circular choruses' normally means dithyrambic choruses in honour of Dionysos; that this interpretation is right is shown by a red-figure vase (37) with three old satyrs (or rather men dressed as satyrs) with lyres inscribed 'Singers at the Panathenaia'. The choruses were evidently quite small as the price given (as recorded in a speech by Lysias) for producing such a chorus is 300 drachmai, contrasted with 5,000 drachmai for a dithyrambic chorus at the festival of Dionysos. We must suppose that, because the Athenians enjoyed these choruses themselves, they assumed that Athena did too.

The Great Panathenaia also started with a pannychis and choruses of men and women, and the torch-race probably occurred on the same evening. This was a relay race, and the torches were lit at the altar of Eros in the Academy; they ran from there

37   Dithyramb singers at the Lesser Panathenaia

through the Agora on to the Acropolis where the fire on the altar of Athena was kindled by the winner.

At dawn on the next day the procession set off from the Dipylon gate and crossed the Agora by the Panathenaic Way to the Eleusinion. The procession is illustrated on the frieze of the Parthenon (p. 139). The peplos was a tapestry with a picture of the battle between the Gods and Giants, in which Athena took a prominent part: this established the rule of reason, represented by Zeus and Athena, over the rule of force. (The theme recurs, as we shall see, twice in the sculpture of the Parthenon.) The peplos was spread over the mast of a ship mounted on wheels (probably this idea was borrowed from the ship-car of Dionysos, to which we shall return). At the Eleusinion the procession must have been reorganised for climbing the Acropolis. The ship on wheels could not make the climb, and it is doubtful if the cavalry could. A sacrifice was made at two altars on the Acropolis, and the new peplos was given to Athena.

The rest of the festival consisted of athletic and musical contests. The prizes for the athletic contests were the special jars of oil from the sacred olives, which have already been discussed. The contests certainly included a foot race, horse-races, a chariot-race, wrestling, boxing, long jump, javelin, diskos and the race for men in armour, and the events had separate classes for men and boys. Then, as at the Little Panathenaia, there were war-dances; each phyle entered a team. For a long time these contests were held in the Agora: the name for the Panathenaic Way is dromos, which means race-course or track, but in the fourth century a special stadium was built for them.

The idea of pleasing a god by contests of song is very old, so that music and poetry were naturally included in the great Athenian festival. Perhaps these contests also were originally held in the Agora, but after the Persian Wars a special concert-hall was built: the model was the Royal Tent of the Persian king, which had been captured. This Odeion was on the south side of the Acropolis, next to the theatre of Dionysos (68).

The prizes were money, but the potters provided unofficial Panathenaic amphorae with pictures of musicians, which probably were bought as souvenirs. There were competitions in solo singing to the lyre, solo singing to the flute, and playing the lyre and flute. But perhaps the most interesting to us is the contest of rhapsodes:

86

these were reciters of epic, and they took turns to recite the *Iliad* and the *Odyssey*. One is illustrated on a red-figure vase (*38*): a bearded man standing on a platform elegantly draped in a large cloak; from his open mouth comes the beginning of a hexameter line. The great importance of this competition is that the Athenians had the opportunity of hearing a professional performance of the *Iliad* and the *Odyssey* every four years.

38   Rhapsode

The festivals of Dionysos show a similar mixture of Holy Day and holiday. As with Athena's festivals, the older festival, the Anthesteria, held in February, shows more primitive ritual, and in the newer festival, the City Dionysia, held in March, holiday predominates. We have noticed already that children took part in the spring festival, the Anthesteria, when they reached the age of three. To compare this to 'confirmation', as has been done, is excessive, but it is true that at the Anthesteria the children were associated with a religious rite which aimed at the renewal of life in the spring and also concerned the dead. The festival had three days called the Opening of the Jars (Pithoigia), the Jugs (Choes), and the Pots (Chytroi). On the first day the new wine was mixed with water in honour of Dionysos and drunk; 'then they sang songs to Dionysos, dancing and calling him Euanthes (flowering) and Dithyrambos and Baccheutas and Bromios'. Two red-figure vases have been associated with this festival, and illustrate the two stages. On the first Dionysos is represented by a mask and a robe draped on a pole (*39*). In front of him is a table from which the wine is being dispensed by women—the wild women, the Maenads, who in the depths of the winter danced with torches on the mountains and tore animals to eat them raw, thus taking into themselves the new life of the god. The vase-painter is saying that the Dionysos of the Anthesteria, the god of vegetation (hence the pole, which on

87

39   Maenads dispensing wine

some similar vases is a tree), is also the god of the Maenads. It is at least likely that the Maenads were the subject of the songs at the Anthesteria. The mask, which is here nailed to the pole to represent Dionysos, could also be worn by a priest who would thereby impersonate Dionysos and by sympathetic magic cause the god to do what his worshippers wanted.

The other vase (*18*) shows a chorus and its poet singing before a kind of maypole. This maypole is decorated with ivy-leaves, the singers wear ivy-wreaths, and one of them holds a spray of ivy. The text for this has rightly been seen in a dithyramb written by Pindar: 'Hither to my chorus, Olympian gods . . . as Zeus sends me to the ivy-giving god, whom we mortals call Bromios.' The chorus on the vase are singing a dithyramb, and the maypole shows that it is a spring dithyramb, at the Anthesteria.

The second day of the festival had three major moments. Dionysos was brought through the streets on a ship on wheels (this was the model for the ship carrying the peplos at the Panathenaia). The god of fertility has to return to re-fertilise the earth; there is no need to ask where he comes from; he returned convincingly if he came by sea. In this return the god was perhaps impersonated by the King Archon wearing Dionysos' mask. The second moment is the marriage of Dionysos to the wife of the King Archon: she is called for this purpose Basilinna, Queen.

They went in a carriage from the shrine of Dionysos to the Boukoleion, which had originally been the office of the King Archon. So this holy marriage ensures fertility for the coming year, and is celebrated by the third great event, the drinking competition which gave the day its name, the Jugs. On the third day the dead were given their offerings in pots (chytroi). The relation of this day to the earlier two days is unclear. But the connection between Dionysos and the dead is very old, and initiation into the rites of Dionysos would secure a better life after death. Only we have no evidence whether this was somehow emphasised in the chytroi.

For the newer festival, the City Dionysia, Dionysos also returned but by land instead of sea. The story of this cult, which was probably introduced in the late seventh century, is as follows: Pegasos of Eleutherai, about 20 miles north-east of Athens, tried to bring the cult of Dionysos Eleuthereus (of Eleutherai) to Athens; the Athenians refused to have it; they all became impotent; they asked the oracle at Delphi what to do and were told to accept the cult. How much is true we do not know. At least we can say that the new cult was probably introduced to meet a crisis, and we know that representations of male genital organs were carried in the procession (as in many other rites in honour of Dionysos). Beyond this, the City Dionysia is holiday rather than Holy Day.

The temple of Dionysos Eleuthereus was built in the sixth century under the south-western slope of the Acropolis. Before the festival, the statue was taken out to a little shrine near the Academy. On the evening before the festival, it was brought back in torchlight procession, thus re-enacting the original introduction. The first day of the festival started with a procession to the temple and a sacrifice of a bull there, followed by the competition of dithyrambs. Each of the ten phylai sent in one chorus of 50 men and another of 50 boys. The producer (choregos) for each chorus was a rich man nominated by the phyle and accepted by the Eponymous Archon: the cost might run to 5,000 drachmai. The producer chose the poet and the flute-player. The first prize for the poet was a bull, the second an amphora of wine, and the third a goat. The victorious chorus won a tripod, a cauldron of bronze with three legs and ring-handles. The tripod was dedicated to Dionysos. Sometimes it was the centre-piece of an elaborate

40 Monument of
Lysikrates

building like the charming monument of Lysikrates (*40*) erected in 334 after a victory with a boys' chorus.

We know very little about the songs because, as early as the fourth century BC, any narrative choral song might be called a dithyramb, and where we are certain that we have a dithyramb, we do not know for what festival it was composed. Pindar, in the dithyramb mentioned above, which seems to have been composed for the Anthesteria, says that Zeus is sending him 'a second time' to Dionysos: the first time may have been the dithyramb recorded for 497; later still was the dithyramb in which he spoke of the Athenians laying down 'the shining foundation of freedom' in the Persian Wars. The songs must have been short to allow the 20 teams to perform in the day. Bacchylides, who was a younger contemporary of Pindar, wrote a poem for the Athenians called after Io, who was an ancestor of Semele, the mother of Dionysos. It is only 50 lines long, and may well have been written for the Greater Dionysia. The short length did not stop its being complicated metrically, and metrical complication carries with it complication of the dance-steps in which the large chorus had to be trained. At the end of the day there was a komos, a torchlight revel, in honour of Dionysos.

The next three days of the festival were given over to drama (*41*). We have to make a major act of adjustment to think ourselves into the Athenian mood for drama. This is what happened. When the archon took office at the beginning of July, he chose three rich men (choregoi) to produce the tragedies, and five rich men to produce the comedies at the next City Dionysia. He also chose three tragic poets and five comic poets out of those who submitted to him plays (or perhaps outlines of plays). It was presumably he who allotted each dramatist a troupe of three actors since the choregos was primarily concerned with the chorus. The comic poets each produced a single comedy, but the tragic poets each produced three tragedies and a sort of gay epilogue, which was called a satyr-play because the chorus were satyrs, the wild followers of Dionysos with goat-ears and horse-tails. The actors wore masks and therefore could take more than one part and it was possible to have supers, who were normally silent but could speak a line or two if required. Scenery was of the simplest (*42*): in the fifth century the audience saw the circular dancing-floor (orchestra), on which the chorus performed and the single central door of the stage building; the wall between it and the side entrances carried panels which could be changed between plays but not between acts: there was a set for tragedy with buildings, a set for satyr-play with rocks and vines, a set for comedy. Presumably the set for satyr-play could be used also for a tragedy or comedy which

41   Theatre of Dionysos

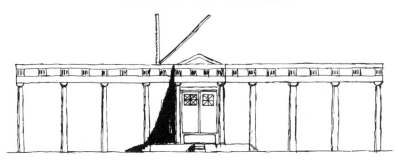

42 Theatre of Dionysos: elevation of stage-building

played in the country. The wall of the stage-building concealed the changing-rooms, the passages connecting the central door with the entrances from the wings, the staircase to the roof, the machinery for the crane (mechane) which was used for flying figures, and the ekkyklema, a platform on wheels which could be rolled out through the central door to show an interior tableau.

A red-figure vase gives some idea of what Euripides' *Iphigenia in Tauris* looked like, if we remember that the painter always paints more than he can see (*43*). The picture tells us something about theatre production and has a good many other points of interest. Euripides describes a very elaborate temple; therefore the simple wooden structure comes from the theatre, and not from his description, and it is the only piece of scenery that the painter shows. Therefore when he thinks of the tragic scene he thinks of the central doorway standing on two wide steps, which make the stage. Inside this structure he has put the primitive idol of Artemis, which is to be taken back to Attica (p. 21); a table of offerings stands in front of the idol. The emphasis on the central door has determined the rest of the composition. The next most important figure is Iphigeneia; the sleeved chiton with elaborate decoration is tragic costume. She holds the key of the temple in her left hand and her letter home in her right hand. She is balanced by her attendant on the right who holds a libation bowl and tray of offerings.

The centre of this composition with its verticals is thus fixed, but the painter wished to say that Iphigeneia gave the letter to Pylades (*I.T.* 725 ff.), that by this means Orestes was recognised, and that Thoas, the barbarian King of Tauris, tried to prevent their escape with the image of Artemis. To bring the three extra figures into the

92

scheme they have to be seated. Landscape is beginning to interest
painters at this time; besides the rocks, against which the flowers
can be seen, there are wavy white lines with flowers rising from
them, but they do not appear in a photograph; perhaps the painter
recalled the moment when the herdsman saw Orestes and Pylades
sitting on the shore (*I.T.* 264), and was encouraged by this to
introduce rocks and flowers. The herdsman himself is probably the
young barbarian with his hand raised in astonishment, who is in
the top left-hand corner of the picture. Orestes and Pylades do not
wear tragic costume, and this is a hint that their sitting position
does not come from the letter-scene. Once this has been realised
the painter becomes intelligible. Pylades receives the letter. Orestes
watches what is going on. But how was the later active intervention
of Thoas to be shown? Orestes turns round in the middle of
supplicating Thoas to watch Pylades, or rather only his left hand
belongs to the supplication. In fact, of course, he never supplicated
Thoas, but this suppliant hand was the only way in which Orestes
could be brought into connection with Thoas; Thoas wears tragic
costume and an Oriental tiara. Behind Thoas is a fan-bearer, and to
balance on the other side a woman in decorated dress, who perhaps
represents the Greek women of the chorus, unless she is Artemis,
the goddess sitting above her temple.

43   Euripides, *Iphigenia in Tauris*

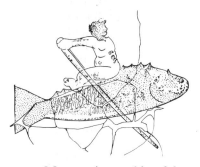

44   Man rowing on blue fish

We have also a number of vases with pictures of comedy. Comic actors wore masks, tights and padding under their tights. The tights were their acting skin and supported the phallos of the male characters (*50*), which was visible except when they wore large cloaks to cover it: they were a reminder that the whole performance was originally a fertility rite. But in the second half of the fourth century the phalloi were made much smaller and in the last quarter of the fourth century male characters, even slaves, wore respectable chitons stretching to their knees. In the fifth century choruses were often dressed as birds or animals. An amusing jug from the Agora shows a man rowing a large blue fish with long oars, and we know of a comedy with a chorus of fish (*44*). Perhaps the chorus came in on stilts (the long oars) and the fish swung beneath them.

Most tragedies and comedies seem a long way from Dionysos, and their performance at his festival is an instance of the Greek view that the god enjoys what his worshippers enjoy. But it is perhaps possible to maintain that there are two sorts of emotional sequence in these plays which do have something to do with Dionysos as the god of new life in the spring. The one, which is the type of comedy, is a sequence of trouble, resistance, intrigue, triumph and marriage, and here the archetypal story, which is obviously a myth of the release of the fruitful earth in the spring, is the story of how Hephaistos bound Hera (an earth-goddess) in a chair and refused all attempts to bring him back to release her until Dionysos brought him back by making him drunk, and then he released her on the promise that he should marry Aphrodite. The other story, which I believe was in the same way archetypal for tragedy, is the story, or rather group of stories, in which Dionysos and his Maenads are resisted by a king on whom Dionysos takes a tremendous vengeance. In origin the story is probably the translation into myth of the idea that the resurgent life of the new year has to meet enormous resistance from natural forces which it ultimately conquers and destroys.

Thus both forms of drama go back to a myth which ensures the fertility of the earth in spring and is therefore in the Greek sense religious, but what survives after centuries in tragedy and comedy is simply the sequence of emotions derived from the two very different myths embodied in quite different material. In tragedy the resistance story itself survives in a number of plays of which the one complete example is Euripides' *Bacchae*, but most other tragedies on themes which have nothing to do with Dionysos show the essential rhythm. In comedy we know also that several poets treated the story of the return of Hephaistos, but again what we have over and over again is a story which ends in marriage but the marriage only comes at the very end when an obstacle or obstacles have been overcome in ingeniously contrived ways. It is the sequence of emotions rather than the story itself that survives, but the sequence of emotions is derived from the story and the story was originally intimately connected with spring ritual.

I said earlier that we have to make a major act of adjustment to think ourselves into the Athenian mood for drama. It is not only the difficulty of accepting a completely different set of dramatic conventions. That can be done fairly easily. More important is the difference between a religious festival and a commercial entertainment. Up to a certain level the Greeks reacted as we do: they hissed the bad actor, they barracked at the new music, they caught a political allusion, they remembered words and tune of a successful chorus. But it would probably be right to say that because drama was performed only at a religious festival, the performance of drama was a privileged occasion in a sense that performance in a commercial theatre can scarcely ever be. At its simplest this means that the Athenian could not choose among a number of entertainments: he took what he was given. At the City Dionysia he was given the plays of three tragic poets and three (or five) comic poets. Certainly the audience's applause was a major factor in awarding the prizes to these poets. But what we should like to know and do not know is what influenced the archon of the year in choosing the poets for next year's festival. The only principle that we can observe is that once established a poet produced over and over again: the three great tragedians averaged roughly a production every other year. We have also to remember that tragedies were never fictional. They were about the great figures of the distant past (except for the two plays at the beginning of our

95

period about the Persian War). And probably at least one of the great figures in any play had a religious cult if not in Athens, then in some city well known to the Athenians. They were people whom the Athenian had grown up to think of as examples, and he went to the theatre to see a reinterpretation of these examples. This is, I think, the grain of truth in Plato's fear that people may model their lives on what they saw on the stage. (Two heroes who particularly interested the Athenians are discussed in Chapter 5.)

Comedy of course was quite different: in the fifth and early fourth century its characters could be fictional, real, mythological or divine, all equally mercilessly caricatured. Again the choice of poets lay with the archon, again it is observable that the established poets were chosen again and again. For the fifth and early fourth century we know most about Aristophanes because he is the only comic poet of whom we have complete plays. But we have a great many fragments of other contemporary comic poets, and as far as we can see the victims of their caricature are the same: the radical politician, the imperialist, the war-monger, the sophist, the modern musician, the modern poet. The uproarious humour, the sparkling wit, the imagination, the phantasy, the verbal and metrical dexterity, the lyricism of Aristophanes are supreme, and this is what makes him still a delight to read. As a political and social critic, he is sympathetic when he attacks the war-monger and champions the independence of the small man, much less sympathetic when he attacks Sokrates and Euripides or praises the old education. But this was what the public wanted, and what the archon chose as suitable for Dionysos' festival.

5

Athenian attitudes to myth

Greek mythology for us is a collection of stories, remote, beautiful or terrifying, which writers and artists can use for very different purposes. Think for instance of Freud's Oedipus complex (a convenient shorthand because the name implies excessive enmity to father and excessive affection from mother), Eugene O'Neill's *Mourning becomes Electra* (a transposition of the Agamemnon story into modern American life), Jean Anouilh's *Antigone* (a modernisation of Sophocles' *Antigone* as a play of the resistance movement in occupied France), Goethe's *Iphigenie*, Racine's *Phèdre*, and a great deal else.

But how did the Greeks and more particularly the Athenians of the Classical Period think of their own mythology? Here one has to distinguish between the period when myths were created, and the period when myths were retold or repainted for the poet's and artist's new contemporary purposes. In fact, the two periods cannot be sharply divided because new myths were continually being created, and retelling or repainting is of course itself an act of creation. But new myths were created round existent figures of mythology, and the great figures of mythology were already established in the Mycenaean age, and further the Mycenaean age appeared to all subsequent Greeks as a remote, beautiful, and sometimes terrifying world, which had vanished except in so far as it was preserved or imagined by successive generations of poets and artists.

But can we define more nearly what we mean by the creation of Greek mythology? Professor Rose's excellent handbook classifies Greek myths as true myths, sagas, and *märchen*. These three names all tell us something about the creation of myths. A true myth is an explanation of some natural process made in a period when such explanations were religious and magical rather than scientific. It is extremely important that after the cold barren winter the earth should be released and bear her fruit. A number of myths, more or less closely connected with ritual, represented this process, as we have seen in the last chapter.

Saga means myth about historical events. The stories about the Trojan War can be claimed as saga, if we accept the evidence that Troy VIIA was sacked by Mycenaeans. The labours of Herakles are saga if, as has been suggested, the wild animals he overcame are the heraldic animals of places over which the King of Mycenae claimed overlordship—the lion of Nemea, the hydra of Lerna, the bull of Crete, the boar of Erymanthos in Arcadia, and the cattle of Geryon in the west, which may recall Mycenaean western adventures. Another extremely attractive suggestion is that the curious story of Herakles' birth goes back to the birth of an Egyptian pharaoh and that the Mycenaeans borrowed the Egyptian belief that the heir to the throne (though in fact his father was the reigning king) was officially the son of a god, who impersonated the reigning king. So the god Zeus took the shape of Alkmene's husband Amphitryon to seduce Alkmene, who became the mother of Herakles. Such a story, misunderstood or wilfully misrepresented by people who had forgotten that kings ever claimed divine ancestry, could easily become the subject of tragedy or comedy. Euripides wrote a tragedy on the Alkmene story. Amphitryon arrived back to find his wife Alkmene pregnant; she had had no means of distinguishing Zeus from her husband; Amphitryon assumed that his wife had been seduced by a rich lover. He threatened to kill her, and when she took refuge on an altar, proposed to burn her off. Zeus quenched the fire by a sudden thunderstorm, which terrified Amphitryon; and Herakles was safely born. Euripides recast the old story into a modern drama of a returning soldier who finds that his wife has been unfaithful.

The third type of myth is the *märchen* or 'fairy story without fairies', because the Greeks did not have fairies. Most of these are, I believe, either poetic embroideries on myth (in the true sense) or on saga, or misinterpretations either of earlier stories or of works of art.

The story of Theseus and Crete is saga. In the second millennium the King of Crete may really have demanded a tribute of boys and girls from the Athenians, and a brave young Athenian

45   Theseus and Minotaur

may really have killed the king and released the Athenians from this need. But the story, as we know it from sixth-century Athenian vases and later literature and art, has three elements of *märchen* and one of religion. The elements of *märchen* are first the Minotaur. The son of the Cretan King Minos, half-bull and half-man, whom Theseus killed, and all the stories that grew up round him, may be *märchen* in the sense that someone early misinterpreted a picture of a Minoan king performing some religious rite in a bull mask, as a monster half-bull, half-man (*45*). More obvious elements of fairy-story are the means by which Ariadne, Minos' daughter, ensured Theseus' success against the Minotaur: the magic wreath, presented to her by Dionysos, which illuminated the dark labyrinth in which the Minotaur lived, and the ball of thread which enabled Theseus to find his way out again.

Theseus then carried Ariadne off on his ship and abandoned her asleep on Naxos, where she was found by Dionysos. But this, as was suggested above, is myth in the religious-magic sense. Ariadne is the earth-goddess, who is awakened in the spring by the fertility god. For many Athenians this Holy Marriage of Dionysos and Ariadne was a great religious fact, a guarantee not only of the fertility of the earth but also of a better after-life for themselves if they worshipped Dionysos right. But on the level of myth in the modern sense, a story about their national hero Theseus in Mycenaean times, the abandonment of Ariadne was discreditable to Theseus. A drastic solution is shown on a red-figure vase painted rather after 470 (*46*). Here there is no moral problem. The lovers are parted by Athena and Dionysos. They look longingly at each other, but Athena drives Theseus off, while Dionysos comes up to

99

46   Theseus and Ariadne

seize Ariadne. To fight the power of the gods is impossible
for mortals. Euripides took quite a different line in a tragedy
called *Theseus*. Enough survives of the fragments to show that
he saw it as a human story, in which Ariadne betrayed her
father, her brother and her country for love of Theseus, and
Theseus (not wholly unlike Jason in the *Medea*) accepted her
help and then rejected her love in pursuit of his Athenian
career: as so often in Euripides the realistically treated story was
put back on its mythological tramlines by Athena in an epilogue
speech which foretold that Ariadne would be found by Dionysos
on Naxos.

   We shall never be able to say anything very precise about the
period in which myths were created. We can only see ways in
which they may have been made, some to explain the processes of
nature, some to recall historical persons or events, some borrowed
from other peoples, whether their original significance was under-
stood or not, some arising from misinterpretation of works of art,
some inventions by the poets. For the classical Greeks (and for us)
the epic poets Homer and Hesiod in the late eighth century represent the first great codification of mythology about gods and
heroes. By then the Mycenaean age was remote, beautiful and
strange: the main lines of the stories had become fixed, and Homer

and Hesiod gave them to the world in written poetic shape for artists to represent and writers to reinterpret.

Let us take Herakles as an example. The main conception in the sixth century was that he was a great fighter who pacified the world for mankind and was finally installed on Olympos as a reward for his labours: in Athens, at any rate, the goddess who protected him in all his labours and introduced him to Zeus at the end was Athena. It was nice to have pictures of him on drinking vessels at a dinner party: one would like to feel oneself a new Herakles. Pictures of Herakles' exploits far outnumber any other mythological scene on black-figure vases. We have extraordinarily little literature to put beside this wealth of archaic illustration, but a papyrus published in 1967 allows us for the first time to reconstruct a long archaic poem about Herakles. The poet is Stesichoros, who composed choral lyric poetry in Sicily in the early sixth century. His work was well known in Athens and was still being sung at symposia during our period. This was a choral song about Herakles' capture of Geryon's cattle: Geryon was a triple-bodied monster who lived in the far west. The papyrus is desperately fragmentary, but it is possible to establish the general sequence of events and some details in a poem which must have run to at least 1300 lines, divided into triads consisting of nine-line strophes and antistrophes and eight-line epodes.

At the beginning Zeus warns Herakles not to go against Geryon, and Herakles answers that he must take what is coming to him. Herakles then has to get to the far west where Geryon lives: to do this he threatens the Sun with his bow and forces him to allow him to use the golden bowl which brings the Sun back from his place of setting in the west to his home in the east, from which he rises next morning. Herakles uses the bowl for the western journey, and 'over the waves of the sea he comes to the lovely island of the gods where the Hesperides have their golden homes. . . . And the Sun, child of Hyperion, got into the golden bowl to cross the Ocean and reach the depths of dark, holy Night, to his mother, wedded wife, and dear children. But Herkales, son of Zeus, went into the laurel-shady grove.' He first met Eurytion, Geryon's herdsman, who had been born 'in a cave by the silver-rooted springs of Tartessos'. Eurytion fell to an arrow from Herakles' bow, and his faithful fierce dog, Orthros, was clubbed to death; so Herakles captured the cattle. Geryon's mother, Kallirrhoe, appealed to him not to fight. But Geryon resisted her appeal and prepared for battle. Herakles decided to attack Geryon by stealth; he took off his shield and helmet, and took his bow and arrows which were anointed with the poisonous hydra's blood. (This is the origin of the tradition that Stesichoros first portrayed the robber Herakles armed only with lionskin, club and bow.) 'Stealthily the arrow pressed on Geryon's forehead, and split his bones and flesh, as the gods decreed. It pressed through to the top of his head, and fouled with purple blood helmet, breastplate, and gory armour. His neck lolled down sideways like a poppy-head.' So one body of Geryon is dismissed. The vase-pictures suggest that Herakles closed with the sword to kill either the second or the third body. Here the papyrus deserts us, but we know from a quotation from the poem that Herakles feasted with the Centaur Pholos on his return. I have described this poem at some length to try and give some of the quality of the leisurely archaic story-telling, which, although it is lyric in form, metre and music, is completely epic in style and contains many reminiscences of Homer.

This is the Herakles whom the archaic Athenians enjoyed, and his two best known festivals, at Kynosarges (where the gymnasium was) and at Marathon, included a great feast, which surely symbolised the completion of his labours. Only at the end of the archaic period can something beyond the strong man's exploits be seen: about 515 the Attic vase-painter Euphronios painted the

47–8 Labours of Theseus

battle of Herakles with the Libyan giant Antaios, If the giant lost
contact with his mother Earth he was doomed; this is, of course, a
contest of strength, but Euphronios has emphasised the untidy
mass of the giant with his straggling hair and beard in contrast
with the beautiful training and neat hair of Herakles. This is not
only a contest of strength; it is also an opposition of civilisation and
barbarism. So Pindar describing Herakles' battle with Antaios
describes the hero as small in stature but great in spirit.

In spite of his many shrines in Attica no one would pretend that
Herakles was a genuine Athenian hero, and the Athenians prided
themselves on their purity of blood. The local Athenian hero,
Theseus, had considerable exploits to his credit, including the
killing of the Minotaur. The Ariadne story, as we have seen, was
also old. So was the story of his rape of Helen (p. 20), and the
story that he helped his friend Peirithoos against the Centaurs
when they tried to make a rough-house at his marriage with a
Lapith princess. Some time about 520 a new poem was written
which set him up as an Athenian Herakles, partly by associating
him with Herakles in some of his exploits like the first Trojan War
and the battle against the Amazons, partly by giving him a series
of duels with giants on his journey to Athens from Troizene,
where the Athenian princess Aithra bore him: a series obviously
modelled on Herakles' battles with monsters, but it is characteristic
of the new attitude of the late sixth century that (although the

48

Krommyan sow and the bull of Marathon are included) they conceive of danger mostly in terms *not* of dangerous animals but of monstrous men: Prokrustes, who chopped or stretched his victims so that they fitted on his bed, Sinis, who tied them to a springy pine tree, Skeiron, who threw them backwards into the sea, where a turtle waited to devour them. Many vases show these scenes (*47–8*), and they so impressed the imagination that the places are still pointed out today.

The popularity of Theseus carries on into the fifth century. As we have seen, in 475 his bones were brought back from Skyros, where he died; and a shrine was built to him in the Agora with dining rooms where feasts could be held to honour him (again like Herakles). For Sophocles in the *Oedipus Coloneus* and for Euripides in the *Supplices* Theseus is the ideal ruler of Athens, who cannot be persuaded by the threat of force to give up a suppliant. In the *Supplices* particularly he appears as the intelligent ruler who believes in the progress of civilisation and gives the maximum of influence to the middle classes: this is about as far as a tragic poet can go in depicting a heroic king as a democrat. In the fourth century, as we shall see, Theseus was certainly regarded as the founder of Athenian democracy, and I suspect that in the late sixth century it was Kleisthenes, the second founder of the Athenian democracy, who was behind the new poem setting Theseus up as a second Herakles. He felt that the new Athens needed its own national hero. But with typical Athenian good sense Theseus did not supplant Herakles; he had his own new exploits and he shared some exploits with Herakles. The visible sign of this is the sculptured metopes of the Athenian treasury at Delphi in the late sixth century: they are shared between Herakles and Theseus. So also in the late fifth century, as we have seen, Herakles and Theseus shared the sculptural decoration of the Hephaisteion. And probably at about the same time as the new Theseus poem, they created a myth, as we have seen, that Herakles, although a foreigner, had been initiated into the Eleusinian Mysteries before going down to fetch Kerberos from the underworld.

A little before the middle of the fifth century the temple of Zeus at Olympia was rebuilt, and the designers of the sculpture were almost certainly Athenians. Here Herakles was very much at home: he was a son of Zeus; the spoils which he had won in the

first Trojan war had enriched the temple, and he was the founder
of the Olympian games. The six square sculptured metopes at
each end of the temple were admirable fields for Herakles' duels
with monsters, and it may be these sculptures in particular which
canonised the twelve labours as the labours of Herakles. I only
want to call attention to three of these twelve metopes. The first
one is Herakles and the Nemean lion. The artist has an entirely
new conception of this story. Herakles here is a beardless boy and
he is very tired: a very young Athena looks on with sympathy. The
artist seems to be saying that this is the beginning of a long career
of trouble.

The second metope shows Herakles fighting Geryon. It may be
an exaggeration to see a brutal force in Herakles here, which does
not appear in the earlier Geryon scenes: he is crashing down with
his club on a Geryon who falls before him. The artist may have
known a famous choral lyric by Pindar, which was quoted by
Herodotos and later by Plato. There are two places where Pindar
criticises Herakles' action against Geryon. This is a surprising new
development in Herakles' story. In a dithyramb (perhaps written
for the Thebans) Pindar says, 'Compared with Herakles, I praise
you, Geryon, but what Zeus does not like, may I commit to
complete silence.' This is his typical way of breaking off an unsavoury story about the gods or heroes. In the other lyric (we have
no evidence for what occasion it was written) the quotation given
by Plato reads, 'Nomos, the king of all, mortal and immortal,
leads with sovereign hand to the justification of violence. I infer
this from the deeds of Herakles.' A papyrus published in 1961
gives the continuation: 'For he drove the oxen of Geryon to the
Cyclopeian door of Eurystheus without asking for them or buying
them, and he stole the terrible mares of Diomede, after over-
coming the King of the Kikones by the Bistonian lake, the
wondrous son of bronze-shirted Enyalios, who withstood him, not
from pride but from valour. For it is better to be killed preventing
robbery than to be a coward.' Then Pindar describes how
Herakles broke in at night, seized a groom and threw him to the
mares, so that he was able to catch them while they were busy
tearing the groom to pieces; 'the King leapt from his bed. . . .'
Here there is a gap in the papyrus of not less than four lines and
not more than 17. When the text starts again we have a reference
to a twelfth labour of Herakles, on which he was sent alone, while

Iolaos buried Herakles' mortal father, Amphitryon, in Thebes. There is no doubt about the tone of the description: Herakles robbed Geryon (and killed him and his herdsman); Herakles robbed Diomede and killed him and his groom. What is the Nomos which justifies this? Nomos is custom, religious belief and law. Somehow the solution must have been given at the end of the poem. We can only guess. Probably the twelfth labour was the last labour, and probably it was either the theft of Plouton's hound, Kerberos, or the search for the golden apples of the Hesperides. Then the burial of Amphitryon is introduced. Does this mean that the burial of Herakles' mortal father was balanced by the death of Herakles himself, or rather not by his death but by his introduction to the gods in Olympos? Is this immortal future what justifies Herakles and does Pindar mean by Nomos our religious belief in him as an immortal, which exists in spite of Herakles' violence?

We have seen already how embarrassing the story of Theseus and Ariadne was to a more moral generation. Herakles, so easily represented as a physical brute, a womaniser and a glutton, was far more embarrassing than Theseus. Euripides treated the psychology of violence in the *Hercules Furens*, which he produced probably in 414. There was an old story of Herakles going mad and killing his children by Megara of Thebes. Euripides links this story to the fetching of Kerberos from the underworld. Herakles returns from Hades to find his human father, Amphitryon, and his wife Megara

and his children about to be put to death by the tyrant Lykos, who is afraid to leave the family of Herakles alive. Herakles proposes to murder Lykos and shows a probably dangerous disregard for his father's caution: 'I'll destroy the new tyrant's house, I'll cut off his unholy head and throw it to the dogs; I'll club to death all the Kadmeians I find disloyal; with my winged arrows I'll fill Ismenos with corpses, and Dirke's white stream shall run red with blood.' He kills Lykos, and the family is preparing a sacrifice to purify the house when Herakles goes mad (*49*); he thinks that

49 Tragic actor
as Herakles

he is driving to Mycenae to kill his taskmaster Eurystheus, he kills his children and his wife thinking that they belong to Eurystheus, and he is just going to kill his father when he collapses, believing that Athena has hurled a rock at him. Finally Theseus, in gratitude because Herakles has brought him safe out of Hades, nurses him back to sanity and persuades him to come to Athens where he will share Theseus' honours. Euripides on the surface gives two interpretations, a mythological and a psychological, madness sent by the jealous goddess Hera, and madness as a reaction to deeds of physical violence—Herakles' father asks him whether the gore of the corpses has driven him crazy, and the messenger evidently thought that Athena only appeared in Herakles' imagination. On this human level Euripides interprets the myth to show that power and wealth (Lykos) is disastrous without morality, that physical strength (Herakles) carries with it the danger of madness, but that friendship (Theseus) is wholly good.

Another old story, or rather two old stories, became intertwined into a tragic story very early. Herakles married Deianeira, the daughter of the King of Kalydon; when they were crossing a river the Centaur Nessos tried to make love to Deianeira as he carried her over. In one version Herakles clubbed the Centaur to death; in the other Herakles shot him with an arrow poisoned with the hydra's blood (this has been identified on an Attic vase fragment which was painted before 650). Before the Centaur died, Deianeira collected some of his poisoned blood. Some years later Herakles visited the city of Oichalia and fell in love with the king's daughter Iole. To get her, he sacked the city and sent Iole back to his home, saying that he would follow himself, when he had made a sacrifice to Zeus: Deianeira could not take this, and sent him as a present a new robe which she had dipped in Nessos' blood, asking him to wear it when he made his sacrifice. He put it on, and in the heat of the sacrifice the poison tore him to pieces. The name of Deianeira ('destroyer of men') suggests that like Klytaimnestra she was a jealous murderess, and so she seems to be in a fragmentary lyric poem by Bacchylides written in the early fifth century.

But about 430 in the *Trachiniae* Sophocles made her a sweet, stupid woman, who believed Nessos when he told her that his blood would be a love-charm to win back Herakles' affections. At that time Sophocles, like Euripides, was deeply interested in the Sokratic problem of the relation of Virtue to Knowledge. Sokrates

50 Comic actor
as Herakles

said that, if you know what is right, you do it. Euripides' Medeia and Phaidra both show and say that passion may decide one to do what one knows is wrong. Sophocles excuses the crimes of his Oidipous, his Phaidra, and his Deianeira by giving them an essential ignorance: Oidipous does not know the identity of his father or mother, Phaidra believes that Theseus is dead, Deianeira thinks that she is using a love-charm. He not only excuses Deianeira but makes her completely sympathetic, and thereby makes himself a new problem, Herakles. This Herakles had killed a man treacherously, sacked a city when its king refused to give him his daughter, and finally sent the daughter home to be his mistress when he arrived. In spite of this, all through the play he has the love of Deianeira and of his son Hyllos and the respect of the chorus as 'the bravest of men'. At the end of the play Sophocles wins our sympathy by a stage-trick. Herakles is brought on dying in agony. We are torn by sympathy with his physical torture, appreciation for his past achievements (which he relates at length), horror at his utter lack of understanding of Deianeira and of his son, admiration for his self-control in physical distress and for his preparations for death. Hyllos, the son, sees in this a great reproach to the gods: Herakles is called the son of Zeus and the gods look on at his sufferings. The chorus see the whole sequence of events, Iole's arrival, Deianeira's sending of the robe, Deianeira's suicide, Herakles' agony and impending death as the will of Zeus. No word is said of Herakles' reception on Olympos, just as at the end of Sophocles' *Electra*, after Orestes has murdered Klytaimnestra and Aigisthos, no suggestion is made that Orestes will be pursued by Furies. In both plays Sophocles brings the curtain down without mentioning the sequel. His Herakles is superhuman in courage and in failings, and Sophocles leaves him at that.

Besides Herakles the slayer of monsters and Herakles the great lover, there is Herakles the glutton. This is an obvious development from the great feasts which he needed to restore his strength after his labours and which were afterwards celebrated in his honour, as we have seen, at Kynosarges and Marathon in Attica by a number of banqueters called parasitoi. Herakles the glutton was a perfect subject for comedy, and he so appears in Aristophanes' *Frogs*. Quite early in the fifth century the Sicilian comic poet Epicharmos described him eating: 'His throat roars, his jaws clash, his molars bang, his dog tooth squeaks, his nostrils hiss, and he waggles his ears.' In the *Frogs* the barmaid and the bakeress loathe him because he stole their wares; and comic actors playing Herakles wore a mask with an enormous mouth, into which they stuck their fingers (*50*). This tradition was also used in the satyr-play. Euripides' *Alcestis* took the place of a satyr-play in his production of 438. Here Herakles arrives on his way to capture the mares of Diomede at the moment when Alkestis has just died. Her husband, Admetos, insists nevertheless on entertaining him in his guest rooms and does not tell him who the dead woman is. Herakles demands an enormous meal and gets roaring drunk, so that the servant, who is mourning Alkestis, complains that they are entertaining a highwayman. Herakles philosophises on the necessity of seizing the pleasures of the day, and then the servant tells him that the mistress of the house is dead. The hedonist immediately turns into the hero, and he goes off to wrestle with Death and win back Alkestis.

I have wandered far from the Olympia metopes. The third metope which I want to discuss is called the Atlas metope. Herakles was sent to fetch the apples of the Hesperides in the far west. In this version he did not go himself: he went to where Atlas (mountain and Titan) was holding up the sky, and he held up the sky while Atlas went to fetch the apples (*51*).

51   Herakles and Atlas, Olympia

52   Herakles and the Hesperides

On the metope Atlas has just returned, and Athena is taking the weight of the sky off Herakles while he and Atlas change positions. I suspect this is a translation of some very old Eastern story, where a giant helps the hero to obtain the fruit of the tree of life.

In the more usual version he goes himself to the nymphs and kills the dragon which guards the golden apple tree. This version appears on a metope of the Hephaisteion. A very pretty picture on a hydria of about 420 also shows it and has two points of interest (*52*). One of the nymphs is called Hygieia 'health'; and evidently the garden of the nymphs is thought of as a magic place where personifications like Health dwell—such a conception formed part of Plato's inspiration when he imagined the Forms of Justice etc. as beautiful women living in a place beyond heaven, or when he thought of Education as a healthy place where the young could dwell receiving fair sights and sounds (p. 169).

Secondly, this Herakles is slim, fine drawn and young—the sort of idealised hero who can consort with nymphs so conceived. Just at this time the sophist Prodikos made a new myth about Herakles: very early Herakles met two women, one plain and sober who was called Virtue (Arete), the other beautiful, made up and magnificently dressed, who was called Vice (Kakia). Each offered him a different life, and he chose the life of toil and virtue, which excluded the pleasures of wine, food and sex. Prodikos' myth is obviously meant as an incitement to the sober life. To choose Herakles for this was not quite so bizarre as it appears. In some accounts Herakles went to heaven immediately after getting the apples of the Hesperides. Athena took him to Zeus and for the rest of time he dwelt on Olympos. This was represented on the east pediment of the Hephaisteion, and there too he seems to have been fine-drawn and young.

53   Herakles driving to Olympos

54   Herakles and the Hesperides

At Olympia he is only young at the time of his first labour; on
the east pediment of the Parthenon he is young but not fine-drawn.
The Meidias painter gives us an idealised Herakles. The story of
his going to heaven with the apples is completely inconsistent with
the story of his being burnt on the pyre on Mount Oita to save
him from the agony of the poisoned shirt. But at about the same
time as the Meidias painter's vase we have the first of a long series
of representations in which Herakles is driven to heaven on a
chariot (53), usually by Athena, and below often appears the pyre
with his armour burning on it. In these pictures, too, Herakles is
often young. Sophocles seems to be thinking of this scene in the
Philoctetes (produced in 409) when he wrote, 'where the bronze-
armoured man approached the gods, flaming with fire, above the
slopes of Oita'. And at the end of the play Herakles himself
appears; he says, 'after all my labours I have the virtue of immor-
tality as you can see'. This is surely the young Herakles. But in the
fourth century this slim young Herakles did not seem to have
enough solidity for so laborious a hero, and another picture of
Herakles among the Hesperides shows a much solider hero,
although he is still young (54). This foreshadows the enormous
beefy Herakles created by Lysippos in the second half of the
fourth century.

I cannot pursue the story further. I have tried to show that once a myth had been created, whether to explain a natural phenomenon, or to record a historical event, or for whatever reason, it became a story which poets and artists could reinterpret according to the needs of their own generation; in fact on this level the history of mythology is simply a part of the history of literature and of the history of art. But a new interpretation does not sweep away older interpretations; they survive side by side with the new, however inconsistent they may be. And for Theseus and Herakles in classical Athens, however many complimentary and uncomplimentary interpretations may be made by poets and artists, worship and cults continue, and that is what matters to the ordinary man; these great heroes of the past may help him in his present trouble.

6

Art and literature

The Strong Style: 480–450 BC

The Persian Wars brought into the open in Athens not only a new awareness that Greeks were distinct from non-Greeks, but also a new relationship with the gods and a new feeling of individual responsibility. The new relationship between gods and men was probably only felt by a comparatively small number of intellectuals and certainly antedates the Persian Wars, but it gets a resounding expression now in the tragedies of Aeschylus and the victor-odes of Pindar. It began late in the sixth century with a philosophical unease at the crimes and adulteries committed by the exceedingly human gods of Homer and with a demand that the divine government of the world should be just. Now this doctrine is loudly stated, with all the rhetoric of superb poetry, in the form that the gods are just and punish human violence in order that men may learn to keep within their own appointed bounds. The other new feeling which again we can trace back to the late sixth century is the feeling that the individual is responsible for his actions and that what matters is neither his family nor his wealth but the purity of his motives. Again this is old doctrine, but this sort of idea probably became somewhat obscured in the aristocratic societies of the seventh century and at the tyrants' courts in the sixth century, when families or etiquette or wealth seemed to be more important than purity of motive. The old idea was revived among the Athenians who established Athenian democracy towards the end of the sixth century, and finds its earliest expression in a poem by Simonides which firmly states that the poet has made the discovery that what matters is that a man should do nothing dishonourable of his own free will: what matters is motive.

Xerxes' invasion of Greece in 480 was an event of such heroic size that in the next ten years it was twice dramatised by Athenian tragic poets, who otherwise restricted their repertoires to stories of the heroic past of the Trojan war period and before. Aeschylus gives the moral in his *Persians*, which was produced in 472. The Persian Wars, and particularly the expedition of Xerxes, demonstrated spectacularly the truth of the old Greek theory that the gods punish violence and pride. In the *Persians* the wise old king Dareios says of Xerxes' disaster: 'Heaps of corpses will give dumb testimony to the eyes of men, even to the third generation, that a mortal should not be too proud. Hybris blossoms and produces a crop of ate, from which it reaps a harvest of tears.' The process has three stages: first, hybris, the initial act of pride, violence or folly; secondly, ate, infatuation, sent by the gods to lead the sinner to his ruin; and thirdly enlightenment, whether of the sinner himself or of the world through his example. Xerxes' act of hybris was in general his naval activities and in particular the bridging of the Hellespont, his ate was to believe the lies which Themistocles told him before Salamis, and his disaster is given to the world as a warning by Aeschylus.

Essentially the same moral is told in Aeschylus' *Oresteia*, which was produced in 458 and told the story of the House of Agamemnon from before the Trojan war to the trial of Orestes by the court of the Areopagos at Athens. Here the old heroic story is tied at the end to a piece of political progress, the establishment of a murder-court to replace an unending sequence of revenges. The kernel of the story and the technique can be seen in the great first chorus, which narrates Agamemnon's murder of his daughter Iphigeneia. The play is set in Argos, and it opens with the watchman on the roof of Agamemnon's palace watching for the beacon, the last in the chain, which will tell him that Agamemnon has captured Troy. The beacon flares out and he shouts to the queen Klytaimnestra to make sacrifice to the gods for the good news. The chorus come in to the central dancing-floor of the theatre, the orchestra. They are the old men of Argos who had been left behind when the expedition went to Troy ten years before, and they enter with a long song in marching rhythm, anapaests, in which they go back to the moment ten years before when the army went to Troy and they were left behind. Now they can scarcely believe the news and want to be relieved of the worry in their minds. When they are established in the orchestra, the metre changes and they sing,

largely in dactyls, of the moment when the host was gathered at
Aulis and the prophet Kalchas, seeing two eagles devouring a
pregnant hare, feared that this signified that the goddess Artemis
was angered and would delay their departure until they had given
her sacrifice. The dactylic metre is used because it was the metre
in which oracles were given. The metre then changes again to
trochaic, and the old men sing that Zeus is the one god in whom
mortals can trust and it is Zeus' rule that men must learn by
suffering, and by their suffering they will learn, against their will
even, what bounds they must keep in their actions. After this hymn
to Zeus, the metre changes again to slower, solemn lyric iambics
to describe the storm which fell on Aulis and prevented the fleet
from sailing. Then Kalchas said that Agamemnon must sacrifice
his daughter Iphigeneia to Artemis. 'When he [Agamemnon] had
put on the yoke of necessity breathing from his heart a changing
wind, impious, unholy, godless, then he changed his mind to
resolve what was utterly daring. For men are made bold by base-
advising, daring madness, which is the beginning of woes. He
dared therefore to become the sacrificer of his daughter, to help
a war to get back a woman and to make an offering before the
sailing of the ships.'

Thus the beginning of the whole chain of events which led up
to Agamemnon's victorious return and his murder by his wife
Klytaimnestra is firmly fixed in Agamemnon's fatal decision to
sacrifice his daughter. It is true that the traditional story allowed
no other end, but that does not for a moment excuse Agamemnon.
It is truer to say that Aeschylus has highlighted this moment of
disastrous decision because, for him, the decision of the individual,
right or wrong, is the whole point of the drama. He has emphasised it by the tremendous build-up of the long and complicated
structure of choral song and dance, and he has put it in a universal

56 Aegina temple:
reconstruction of
west pediment

perspective by inserting just before his narrative the hymn to Zeus, which expounds how the moral government of the universe works. It is difficult in a bald English translation to give any idea of the majestic language and flowing imagery of this passage and the passage quoted from the *Persians*.

This is the strong style of this period, which Aeschylus shares with the lyric poet Pindar, as can be seen from a brief quotation of one of Pindar's victor-odes, which were written for athletic champions when they won their victories at one of the great national athletic festivals. My example is chosen from one of the last poems that we have by Pindar, written for a young Aeginetan victor at the games of the Pythian Apollo at Delphi. Pindar has described the misery of the defeated who creep home to their mothers in shame and then he goes on: 'He, having won a brave new thing, in great hope flies in the flower of his youth on the wings of courage, his thought far above wealth. In a moment human joy waxes, so also it falls to the ground, shattered by a swerving judgment. Creatures of the day. What is he? What is he not? A dream-shadow is man. But when heaven-sent brightness comes, clear light is over men and life is honey sweet.' Like Aeschylus he sees the young man and his fabulous momentary happiness against a much wider background of general human happiness and misery. Again, the happiness is the result of a right decision, in fact man is responsible, and again the story is told in staccato style with flashing imagery.

The island of Aegina is only just beyond Salamis. Politically its connections with Athens had been stormy: after a long war with Athens Aegina had taken the Persian side in 490, but had fought magnificently with the Greeks in 480. By the time Pindar wrote this ode, Athens had conquered Aegina and made the island part of the Athenian empire. Whatever the political

differences, the artistic connections between the two neighbours had always been close. The one major monument of sculpture in which the change from the old to the new style can almost be seen happening is the Doric temple of Aphaia on its pine-clad hill at the north-east end of Aegina. The goddess was a local goddess who had affinities with Artemis. Her temple, which was built early in the fifth century, had sculpture in both its pediments, representing a battle between Greeks and Orientals with Athena as the central figure. As Herakles is one of the combatants on the east pediment, that battle is probably the earlier Trojan war, when the Greeks captured Laomedon's Troy and the Aeginetan hero Telamon took part. Then the west pediment probably represents the more famous attack on Priam's Troy, in which one of the leading heroes was Telamon's son, Ajax. It seems likely that the sculptured decoration had some connection with Aegina, but it must be admitted that the connection is a slender one, as nothing distinguishes the Aeginetan heroes from the other Greeks.

We have then two pediments, the west pediment probably rather before, and the east pediment rather after 490. The difference can be seen more easily in the composition than in the style of the individual figures, which have been restored and their surfaces re-worked in modern times. On the east a rhythm of motion runs through the whole pediment (55): on the right side of the pediment the movement runs up the body of the fallen warrior in the corner, down the body and outstretched leg of Herakles, up the leg and body of the man who runs to catch the falling warrior, down the body of the falling warrior, up the right leg and body of his adversary to come to rest in the central figure of Athena. This 'line of force' composition is completely different from the composition of the west pediment (56); there, what is essentially the same subject is represented by two distinct groups on each side of Athena. Each side of the pediment has an outer group of archer, crouching warrior and dying men, turned towards the corner of the pediment, and an inner group of two warriors facing outwards. The static symmetry of the west pediment is archaic; the line of force which holds the east pediment together is the beginning of the strong style.

The line of force can be seen again on contemporary vases. An Athenian red-figure cup which was discovered in the Agora at Athens is a good example (57). The potter Gorgos signed it, and he

57   Achilles and Memnon

probably also painted it; if so, he is the man we know better as
the Berlin painter because he decorated a very fine amphora of
Panathenaic shape in the Berlin museum. On the outside of the
cup he has painted the final duel between Achilles and Memnon
(the Ethiopian king who came to help Priam after Hektor had
been killed). Achilles is urged on by his mother, the sea-goddess
Thetis; behind Memnon his mother, the dawn-goddess Eos, raises
her right hand to implore Achilles, while her left hand tears off
her head scarf. Essentially this is the scheme of the east pediment
of Aegina.

The inside of the cup has a boy, wearing a wreath and with a
knobbly stick in his hand, crouching as he waits to put a racing
hare on the ground (58). As
often, the curve of the picture
frame becomes curved ground
on which his feet rest. The boy's
stick cuts the circle into two
segments, and the curve of the
smaller segment is echoed within the larger segment by the
curve of the boy's body, while
near the edge of the larger
segment, points of interest are
established by the boy's head,
his elbow, the hare, and his
right foot. A contemporary cup

58   Boy with hare

119

59　Boy chasing hare

shows the next moment in the story, the boy has put the hare down and is starting to run after it (59). The general shape of the design is pentagonal, but much of the outline of the pentagon is left to the imagination to supply.

These compositions in a round space have the same kind of dynamic unity as the east pediment of Aegina, but it is applied to a circular instead of a triangular field. Solemnity rather than movement characterises the earliest single figure in the new style. When the Athenians returned to Athens after evacuating it before the Persians in 480, they found much damage on the Acropolis and piled the older statues together in a dump before rebuilding. The latest statues which have been discovered in this dump show the beginnings of the new style. To judge by the style and the lettering of the inscription, Euthydikos dedicated his kore not long before the Persian war. It is one of the numerous marble girls dedicated in gratitude to Athena (p. 22). This kore differs from her predecessors in the simplicity of her drapery and hair, and the pensive brooding expression of the long heavy-lidded eyes and the straight mouth (60). She has a brother in a boy's head also found in the dump; he also is pensive with heavy-lidded eyes and a straight mouth (61). Enough colour remains on his hair to show that it was fair, and it is plaited behind, a fashion which is common for the next 20 years and more. After the long succession of archaic young men with smiling faces, heads and bodies

60　Kore of Euthydikos

upright, marching militarily forward, this pensive head, slightly lowered and slightly turned, is startling. A fragment of body which probably belongs shows that the hips were uneven and one leg was bent, the other straight. For the first time the unity of the figure is emphasised by this uneven stance, which is reflected in the poise of the head. Court manners are gone, and this boy, like the man praised by Simonides, is responsible for his actions. He is probably a young athletic victor.

The strong style is fully realised in the sculpture of the temple of Zeus at Olympia.

61   Fair-haired boy

Olympia, inland from the west coast of the Peloponnese, had been a centre for international athletics since 776. The festival was in honour of Zeus. There were two traditions about the founding of the games in the heroic past: according to one they were founded by Herakles, and according to the other they were founded by Pelops, when he had defeated the local king Oinomaos in a chariot-race for the hand of his daughter, Hippodameia; both traditions have influenced the sculpture. The sculpture had presumably been finished in 457, when the Spartans dedicated a golden shield as the central akroterion, the ornament over the apex of the pediment; but the temple had to wait a quarter of a century for its cult-statue, the great ivory and gold Zeus made by the Athenian Pheidias. The two pediments, each with six metopes in the frieze underneath them, can therefore be dated between 470 and 457.

The temple belonged to Zeus, and Herakles and Pelops were both said to have founded the games. So it is very natural that Herakles should have his place in the six sculptured metopes on each of the short sides, which accommodate his twelve labours (p. 105), and that the chariot-race of Pelops and Oinomaos should occupy the east pediment. But the relevance of the battle between

Greeks and Centaurs on the west pediment is not so obvious, nor why Apollo should preside over it.

Apollo was the son of Zeus and Peirithoos was the son of Zeus. Was this reason enough for making the rough-house at Peirithoos' wedding the subject of the west pediment (62)? It is possible that there was a different kind of connection. Herakles in the metopes is not represented as the founder of the Olympic games but as the son of Zeus who, with the help of Athena, destroyed monsters dangerous to mankind. The battle at the wedding-feast of Peirithoos can be interpreted as an example of the divine law that violence brings disaster and modesty wins. The strong Centaurs could not take their wine and made a rough-house; the disciplined Greeks overcame them, and Apollo may have been introduced to preside over the battle as the son of Zeus who embodied this law, because he has 'know yourself' inscribed outside his temple at Delphi. The designer of the pediment then chose the story because it could be interpreted in the same terms as Aeschylus interpreted the Persian War, and there is something Aeschylean in the framing of the action by anxious watchers in the corners like a chorus and in the dominance of the central god.

If this interpretation is right, it should hold also for the east pediment (63), which will have a meaning beyond the obvious local relevance of the chariot-race between Oinomaos and Pelops for the hand of Hippodameia. Pausanias identifies Zeus in the centre; on the right Oinomaos and his wife Sterope, his charioteer Myrtilos, and the river Kladeos in the corner; on the left, Pelops and Hippodameia, and the river Alpheios in the corner. The other figures he merely calls grooms, but one of them, an old man with his hand to his chin, is rightly interpreted as a seer who foresaw Oinomaos' disaster. The question then is this: were visitors to the temple expected to see here the traditional story that Pelops

63   Olympia:
reconstruction of
east pediment

bribed Myrtilos, Oinomaos' charioteer, to remove the linch-pin
from Oinomaos' chariot and cause him to crash? Or was this a
quite different version in which Oinomaos the proud and violent
king was hurled from his chariot by the thunderbolt of Zeus?
Sophocles in the *Electra* quotes the traditional story; but Pindar
in 476 in his first Olympian Ode makes Pelops pray to Poseidon
for victory over the king, who has already killed 13 of his daughter's
suitors; Poseidon gave Pelops a golden chariot and untiring winged
horses, 'and he overcame the violent Oinomaos'. Pindar sup-
presses the unsavoury Myrtilos story. The killing of Oinomaos
by Zeus' thunderbolt is another variant. In the pediment the
dominant position of Zeus, the fact that he held a thunderbolt,
and the anxiety of the seer, all make this interpretation likely.
Pelops wins because he is modest; Oinomaos loses and perishes
because he is arrogant and violent. Zeus directs the action according to the Aeschylean law that the doer must suffer: the seer (like
Kalchas in the *Agamemnon*) knows what will happen, and the
river-gods in the corners watch like an Aeschylean chorus. This
was possibly the first time that the whole sculptural decoration of
a temple illustrated the theme, god's relation to man, and illustrated it in Aeschylean terms.

The square field of the metopes sets the same kind of compositional problem as the circular field inside a cup, and the
designer has sometimes emphasised the diagonals (bull, horse,
Augeias), sometimes set a triangle (deer, Amazon, boar, Geryon)
or an inverted triangle (Kerberos) against the square. In the Atlas
metope (*51*) the figures are set on the principle that a lesser weight
away from the centre balances a larger weight near the centre:
thus the two perpendiculars of Athena and Herakles supporting
the sky are balanced by Atlas on the extreme right. The groups
are held together by the meeting glances of Athena and Atlas and

64 Athena and Stele

by Atlas' out-stretched hands with the apples.

The Athena is the first female figure that we have seen with stiff leg and bent leg clearly differentiated and with the simple Doric peplos instead of the elaborate Ionian chiton and himation. This solemn Athena has many parallels in this period: the Sterope and Hippodameia of the east pediment are generally similar. A contemporary Attic Athena, leaning on her spear by a stele, is less severe and the drapery is more elaborate (64). The long overfall is divided by a girdle, so that there is a pleasant balance between the part above the overfall, the part below, and the skirts; and the V-folds above the overfall are echoed by V-folds below. The fact that she is usually called the Mourning Athena is a testimony to the solemnity of the style. She may be looking at a casualty list, but others have suggested that she is looking at a boundary stone and that a treaty was engraved below, or that the stele is a turning point for the races, and the relief a dedication by a manager of the Panathenaic games.

Another open-V composition of about 460 is the Pan painter's Artemis and Aktaion (65). The vase is what is called a bell-krater, a comparatively new shape, which with its simple curve and its eminently sensible form for holding water and wine answers the taste of the period: later the lip turns out elegantly, the handles become much larger and curl up, and the simple foot is developed into a kind of pedestal. The artist is given his name from the scene on the back of this vane, Pan chasing a shepherd boy. He is an interesting mixture of archaic, almost archaistic elegance and awareness of modern tendencies. The story that Aktaion, Artemis' favourite huntsman, saw her bathing, may be too late for this picture; probably his offence was that he had made love to Semele, who was loved by Zeus; for whatever reason, the goddess drove his hounds mad, and they tore him to pieces. In the Pan painter's picture the hounds are already at him. Artemis' only favour is to put him out of misery with an arrow as she turns to go. The merits of the composition are obvious. Artemis wears the old-fashioned Ionian dress with elaborate folds on the cross-slung himation and skirt. This is the dress of the marble korai of the Acropolis, which already, by the time of the Euthydikos kore, had been reduced to its simplest form. But Artemis' pose, particularly the frontal foot cutting across the border, is entirely modern; so is the collapsing figure of Aktaion with the frontal legs and the feet skewed round into the front plane. They lead us to a consideration of big painting, but first we must say more about the Olympia pediments.

As a composition the west pediment may be compared with the east pediment of Aegina. Both are dominated by a line of force

65　Artemis and Aktaion. Attic red-figure bell-krater

which now echoes and now rebounds from the slanting line of the top of the pediment, but the Olympia pediment has 19 figures to the 11 of Aegina. The thrust out of the corners is triplicated: two watching women, Lapith. A group of Lapith and Centaur on each side fills the gap between the next upward thrust and the next downward thrust. Thus the earlier simple composition is thickened up, and the positions are far more complicated and the faces more expressive. The east pediment is inevitably much more static. The corners make a balancing block of three figures, and the outside line of the innermost figures (the worried seer on the right) slants against the slant of the roof. Between these corner groups the long horizontals of the two chariots with their attendant figures balance about the five organ pipes of the central figures. The artist had a precedent in the much earlier Siphnian treasury at Delphi and elsewhere for his chariot groups. It is a good balancing composition, but its success is partly due to the psychological tension between the figures: the interest of the river-gods, the concern of the seer for his king, the proud stance of Oinomaos, and the majesty of Zeus. Painters too at this time were interested in the moment before action or the moment after.

The new stance of the standing male figure, which was first seen in the latest figures from the Acropolis dump, the Critian boy and the fair-haired boy (p. 121), is seen in all the standing figures: Apollo, Zeus (but his legs are wrapped in his himation), Oinomaos and Pelops. They all stand with hips uneven and one leg stiff and the other slightly bent. They correspond to the female figures, Sterope and Hippodameia and the Athena of the Atlas metope.

The revolution in sculpture which has been described ran parallel to a revolution in painting. A permanent cross-connection between sculpture and painting was given by the fact that leading painters were employed to colour sculpture, and in the case of the west pediment of Olympia individual groups of Lapiths and Centaurs were inspired by wall-paintings in Athens. The leader of the revolution in painting was Polygnotos of Thasos. In Athens he was very closely connected with Kimon, the son of Miltiades, the victor of Marathon. Kimon was the successful Athenian general of the period after the Persian War and the leading conservative politician. Kimon's sister Elpinike was said to be Polygnotos' mistress, and the tragic poet Sophocles, also a friend of Kimon, was probably painted at least once by Polygnotos.

Polygnotos' pictures can be dated in the second quarter of the fifth century. He painted chiefly in Athens, but his two most famous pictures, the Sack of Troy and the Underworld, were painted at Delphi. In Athens he was associated closely with Mikon, an Athenian painter, who was also a sculptor. In the Stoa Poikile, built by Kimon's brother-in-law Peisianax on the north side of the Agora, he painted a scene from the Sack of Troy (as a gift in return for the grant of Athenian citizenship); Mikon painted an Amazonomachy and, with a third painter Panainos, the Battle of Marathon. Polygnotos also painted in the Theseion and the Anakeion.

Aristotle compares him with Sophocles as skilful in portraying ethos; the word here means something like moral purpose, which suits the solemn figures of this period. Pliny says that he varied the former fixity of expression on the face: this is partly the abandoning of the archaic smile but also the use of three-quarter faces instead of profile and of new angles for the head. It comes out clearly from the description by Pausanias of his pictures at Delphi that he not only painted various new poses, but also abandoned the base-line and dotted his figures over the wall. Thus the revolution in painting includes a new element which is present but not so obvious in the revolution in sculpture, the representation of depth, because Polygnotan figures were set on wavy lines representing ridges one behind the other; the intention to get an impression of depth is certain because some of the figures were half or more than half concealed by the ridges. The procedure is primitive, and later writers thought of Polygnotos as an archaic painter, but it was the first determined attempt to set the figures of a composition into a more consistent and realistic spatial relation to each other than could be achieved by placing them along a base-line.

For the vase-painter with his limited colour range (as long as he used red-figure), his small picture-area, and his curved surface, the revolution was difficult to follow, and the majority adopted the new procedures only in so far as they affected the single figure and were compatible with the retention of the base-line. Some, however, went all the way. The most interesting experiment is a picture (66) by a painter who is called the Niobid painter because the other side of the vase shows Apollo and Artemis shooting down the Niobids.

66   Herakles and heroes

The scene has been variously interpreted as the Argonauts on
Lemnos urged by Herakles to set off; heroes of Attica at the time
of the battle of Marathon; Herakles in the underworld; a recent
most ingenious variation of the last interpretation sees here
Theseus returning from Hades to Athens, when Kimon brought
back his bones from Skyros in 475. The absence of any indication
that the scene is in the underworld perhaps makes the first interpretation, the Argonauts on Lemnos, still the most likely. But this
picture has enough to interest us even if we do not know its
subject. The whole scene consists of eleven figures. A central
triangle of three figures, Herakles, the young man seated on the
rock, and the young man lying on the ground, is framed on one
side by the club of Herakles and the arms of the youth on the
ground, and on the other side by the head and shoulders of
the seated man and the shield below him. The eight figures outside
this triangle are tied to it chiefly by the fact that all except one look
towards it, partly also by the spears which slant outwards from the
centre. The area is divided up by reserved lines which indicate
rocks. The reclining figure is in front, and the shield gives the
width of the area on which he lies. The warrior with the snake on
his shield is a little further back. The next level holds the youth
on the extreme left and Athena. A little further back still are the
helmeted warrior, Herakles, the seated youth, the youth holding
his helmet, the bearded man, and the horse with the boy behind
it. Furthest back is the youth on the left, who is half-hidden by his
hill. This is the kind of grouping which Pausanias describes in

Polygnotos' pictures, and the Niobid painter evidently copied a large painting.

These are great and serious people, who are conscious of their destiny. The painter has used all the new devices of three-quarter faces, lined brows, and complicated poses to express their individuality. The likeness of Herakles to the standing male figures of the Olympia pediments is clear, and the picture was conceived in the same spirit. In the arrangement of the rocky ground, in the stance of the figures, in the detailed treatment of the faces, in the foreshortened shields, the painter has completely and consistently broken away from the archaic conventions which still persisted in the first quarter of the century (and in the work of some artists much longer).

The Classical Style: 450–425 BC

Within the century and a half which separates the Archaic period from the Hellenistic age, the 25 years from 450 to 425 BC has a special claim to be called the classical period since in it were produced the Parthenon, the *Antigone* and *Oedipus Tyrannus* of Sophocles, and the *Medea* and *Hippolytus* of Euripides. Partly the chance of preservation and party the fact that these particular works are well dated makes it desirable to isolate them and treat this 25 years as a period on its own. The *Antigone* was produced shortly before 440, the *Medea* in 431, the *Oedipus Tyrannus* probably in 429 and the *Hippolytus* in 428. Work was begun on the Parthenon in 447; in 438 the gold and ivory statue of Athena was dedicated, so that by that date the roof must have been completed and the frieze blocks either carved or ready for carving; the pedimental sculptures were subsequently put into place, but the work seems to have been completed by 432.

The common conjunction of cold or formal with classical is wildly wrong, as anyone who has seen the *Oedipus Tyrannus* or really looked at the Parthenon frieze must know. The grain of truth in the equation lies in the classical tendency not to suppress emotion but to transmute it into a formal pattern. In contrast to the strong style the classical artist does not operate with massed effects, with violent distortions or with compositions based on lines of force. Instead he works with clear contrasts, with flowing lines, and with balance of masses. In many ways the classical style is a reversion to the ripe archaic manner, with the major difference, however, that all the deep and stormy experience of the last 30 years is contained in the new forms.

Let us look at this new style first in literature. The most obvious difference in the plays of this period is the reduction of the lyrics sung by the chorus and the increase of the dialogue spoken by the actors. One result is that each single play contains more action than before. The unit now is normally the single play and not the connected group of three plays as, for instance, in the *Oresteia* of Aeschylus. It is unfortunate that for no year have we a record of what three plays Sophocles produced together, and we do not know therefore what principles guided him (against a single reference to a *Telepheia*, which should mean three plays on the Telephos story, we can set the known dates of the three Theban plays, *Antigone* before 440, *Oedipus Tyrannus* probably 429, *Oedipus Coloneus* produced posthumously in 401). For Euripides, however, we know the plays produced in 438 and the plays produced in 431. The principle was evidently variation, and the audience, instead of seeing a sequence of three chapters in the same story, saw three very different stories. The three tragedies, for which Euripides won the third prize in 431, were the *Medea*, the *Philoctetes* and the *Dictys*. Very roughly they can be classified as a play about a bad woman (*Medea*), a play about soldiers (*Philoctetes*), and a play about an ill-treated woman (Danae in the *Dictys*).

The unit, then, is the single play, and within the single play the dialogue has greatly increased at the expense of the songs sung by the chorus. In terms of metrical and musical texture, spoken dialogue is now divided into sections by the songs of the chorus, which stand out in clear contrast. The direction had already been established in the later plays of Aeschylus, but even in the *Oresteia* the choruses are still much longer and much more elaborate than in the plays of Sophocles and Euripides. In particular the first chorus, which is always something of a show-piece in tragedy, is in the *Agamemnon*, as I have tried to show, brilliantly built up with over 60 lines of introductory recitative anapaests followed by over 150 lines in lyric metres consisting of six pairs of strophe and antistrophe, whereas the opening chorus of the *Oedipus Tyrannus* consists only of 66 lyric lines in three pairs of strophe and antistrophe.

Besides this difference in texture the style changes: the swift succession of images, some of which run through the play and even all three plays like purple threads, and the tremendous single lines of resounding words have gone; in their place the imagery is much more sparingly applied where it is most effective, and the whole movement of the iambic lines is freer and easier. Positively, Sophocles shows a tendency to give his emotional high-points a definite form, which sometimes strikes the modern ear as mannered and excessive. Ajax' suicide speech (*Aj.* 815 ff.) is the more effective because it is composed of a succession of invocations to Zeus (824), to Hermes (831), to the Furies (835), to the Sun (845), to Death (854), to the daylight (856), and to the natural features of his home and the Trojan plain where he is dying (859).

These are the visible and calculable externals of the new style. They express a whole approach to the ancient stories which is different from the approach of Aeschylus. To put it crudely, Aeschylus was concerned with the nature of divine government, the way in which it worked, and the moment of decision in a human being which put the machinery into action, and he used every available device of spectacle, costume, music and poetic language to impress the solemnity of this interpretation on the audience. The two younger tragedians are much more concerned to show what qualities the ancient heroes must have had if these stories were true. The story is therefore put across more quietly, and the full resources of spectacle and music are reserved for particular moments: the appearance of the self-blinded Oidipous to sing a lyric lament with the chorus at the end of *Oedipus Tyrannus*, or the lyric lament of Hippolytos when he is carried on dying after the wreck of his chariot into the presence of his father Theseus and the goddess Artemis.

It follows that the younger tragedians are far more concerned with displaying character than Aeschylus. Sophocles in particular organises his story into a series of scenes in which the hero is contrasted with a number of subsidiary characters each of whom brings out a different facet in his character. Oidipous and the priest are king and subject; Teiresias the seer represents supernatural knowledge, but Oidipous human skill; Kreon's reasonableness displays Oidipous' angry prejudice; Oidipous and Iokaste are contrasted as man and woman but are held together by their double relationship—Iokaste is somehow shown to be his mother as well as his wife. Euripides uses this technique too, but perhaps

more than in Sophocles his characters display themselves in mono-
logues (usually pronounced before the chorus) and in set debate,
which is a fair description of the arguments between Jason and
Medeia in the *Medea* and between Theseus and Hippolytos in the
Hippolytus. Between these various types of scene the chorus provide
lyric interludes, in which they comment on what they have
experienced, sometimes generalising, sometimes underlining the
emotion.

Both poets present the story in terms of action conducted by
people of a particular sort. But their view of the divine framework
differs widely. Sophocles, as far as we can see, accepts the traditional framework: Apollo is the son of Zeus, his oracles are
therefore true; if he prophesied that Oidipous would kill his father
and marry his mother, this must be accepted; it is no use criticising
Apollo; all that can be done is to show what sort of a man Oidipous
was to bring about the revelation of the truth. Euripides does not
accept the framework so readily. In the *Medea* he can practically
leave it out of account: Jason's selfishness and Medeia's love,
turned sour into jealousy and revenge, provide all the motive
power needed. But in the *Hippolytus* he introduces the gods in
person, Aphrodite at the beginning and Artemis at the end. These
gods, however, have nothing to do with the just government of the
universe. Aphrodite announces that she benefits those who rever-
ence her power and punishes those who proudly resist her;
Artemis can only promise her worshipper Hippolytos that his
death will be avenged by the death of a protégé of Aphrodite and
that he will be honoured as a hero by the maidens of Troizene.

These gods are as spiteful as the worst of humans. The ordinary
spectator might accept them as sub-Homeric. The intelligent
spectator might suggest that they stand for psychological forces in
the characters and that the action of such psychological forces is
ruthless. Aphrodite is sexual desire, and this is an easy and obvious
interpretation. Artemis is more difficult; she may represent
Hippolytos' dedication to a career of hunting and athletics, a
dedication which makes him reject the ordinary pleasures of the
body, including sexual satisfaction, a dedication which expresses
itself in his extraordinarily beautiful prayer to Artemis at the
beginning of the play and his heartbreaking line of farewell to her:
'a long association, but you leave it easily' (1441). Such a dedication could easily be generalised as a psychological force which

drives men in many careers to disregard normal pleasures and normal claims; Ibsen's *Master Builder* certainly contains this element, but we have no knowledge that Euripides took this further step.

To interpret the gods like this was dangerous. In the most obvious sense it might involve the interpreter in a trial for impiety as Anaxagoras had found and Sokrates was to find. From the historical point of view such an interpretation may be adequate for Aphrodite (and, as we shall see later, for Dionysos), but it only covers one side of Artemis and for other gods it is totally inadequate. And there is the further danger that such an explanation may destroy some valuable social element which is contained in the received religion.

This is a problem with which we are familiar today and of which Sophocles, who had no desire to abandon the traditional view of just, divine government, was keenly aware. In the *Antigone* the chorus have heard that someone has buried the body of Polyneikes; Polyneikes had been killed by his brother Eteokles when attacking the city and had him-self killed Eteokles; the new king Kreon had decreed a public funeral for Eteokles and no burial for Polyneikes. The chorus comment on this situation in a lyric, in which they ascribe the growth of civilisation — sea-transport, agriculture, hunting, land-transport, speech, housing and medicine—to the inventive genius of man: 'having beyond all hope a cunning in the contriving of his art, he sometimes goes to good and at other times to bad. If he keeps the

67 Polyneikes and Eriphyle

laws of the land and justice, sworn by the gods, he is high in his city. He has no city, who associates with dishonour for the sake of crime.' The chorus are commenting on the situation that they know—someone has disobeyed Kreon; for the audience the comment is ironical because they know that it was Antigone who buried Polyneikes and that she was obeying an older law than Kreon's decree. But they would inevitably remember the lovely lyric and ponder its more general application.

In the prosperous imperial Athens of the mid-fifth century it was natural to think about the progress of civilisation, and we possess several roughly contemporary accounts which name the same topics in this progress. What distinguishes Sophocles' account is that he ascribes the progress not to gods nor to heroes, like Triptolemos or Prometheus, but to man. This was, I suppose, the normal view of the Sophists in the middle of the fifth century, and the writers and artists themselves were beginning to think that their success was due to their own skill, not to the Muses or to the gods of their crafts, Hephaistos or Athena. So relying on 'the contriving of his art' (techne) Sophocles wrote a book about the chorus; the sculptor Polykleitos wrote a book about his ideal figure; Iktinos, the architect of the Parthenon, wrote a book about architecture, and a little later the painter Parrhasios wrote on painting. Sophocles, however, saw quite clearly the dangers of this reliance on human skill and asserts here firmly that it is only one factor in a successful society: law and justice must prescribe the area in which it works, and the sanction of legal decisions is an oath by the gods.

Perikles, who was the friend of the advanced thinker Anaxagoras, also saw the problem. Thucydides, the historian, has certainly preserved the spirit, if not the actual words, of the speech which he delivered in 431 BC at the state funeral of those Athenians who had been killed in the first year of the Peloponnesian War. The problem for a full democracy, which Perikles had realised for the citizen body of Athenians, was this. Athenian citizens had equality under the law, and Perikles claimed with a good deal of justice that promotion was the reward of merit. Festivals and public buildings gave recreation to the spirit. The most advanced thinkers came to Athens to expound their views, which were often contrary to the received religion and the ethic based on it. The ideal of the Athenian, as Perikles expressed it, was to have the power of adapting himself to the most varied forms of action with the utmost versatility and grace. How was a society composed of highly individualistic, free-thinking amateurs to work?

The simple answer is, of course, that such a society did not exist, that the mass of Athenians went on in the old ways, subject to the old restraints. For a minority the problem undoubtedly did exist. For them Perikles answered: 'we do not transgress the law, because we obey both those men who from time to time hold office, and the laws, particularly those laws which are made for the help of the injured and those unwritten laws which carry with them a disgrace recognised by all.' In fact, this is the same answer that Sophocles had given: the new intelligent, technological, democratic society can only flourish if it operates within the law. Perikles, however, says nothing about the gods, and he grades his restraints into executive acts, laws, and unwritten laws. He means by unwritten laws such things as the right of asylum, the right of burial, and respect for one's elders; Sophocles called them laws of the gods; Euripides called them Hellenic laws, i.e. laws valid in all Greek states; Perikles bases them on the feeling of shame which every transgressor has, a kind of universal conscience.

A universal conscience cannot be painted or sculptured, but if it is put in the terms 'a man must keep within the bounds prescribed by the gods for men' it immediately suggests a number of ancient stories, which Aeschylus and the other tragic poets had interpreted in these terms. It is reasonable to suppose that the designers of the Parthenon were thinking on these lines when they chose the subjects for its sculpture. Certainly when Perikles claimed in the funeral speech of 431 that Athens was an education for Greece, he must have been thinking of the Parthenon which was dedicated in 438 and in 431 was in the final stages of external decoration.

The work for the Parthenon started in 447 as part of the great building programme, which Perikles called 'the educating of Greece', although his opponents said that he was decking out the city like a harlot at the expense of the allies. Pheidias planned the whole operation, as well as being responsible for the gold and ivory cult-statue of Athena in the Parthenon. The programme included the Hall of the Mysteries in Eleusis, the Odeion or concert hall below the Acropolis for the musical competitions of the Panathenaia, the Propylaia or entrance-way to the Acropolis, as well

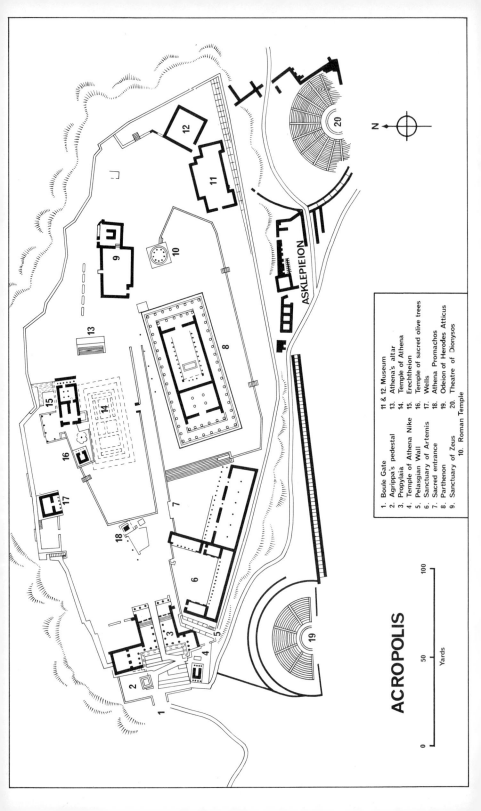

ACROPOLIS

1. Boule Gate
2. Agrippa's pedestal
3. Propylaia
4. Temple of Athena Nike
5. Pelasgian Wall
6. Sanctuary of Artemis
7. Sacred entrance
8. Parthenon
9. Sanctuary of Zeus
10. Roman Temple
11 & 12. Museum
13. Athena's altar
14. Temple of Athena
15. Erechtheion
16. Temple of sacred olive trees
17. Wells
18. Athena Promachos
19. Odeion of Herodes Atticus
20. Theatre of Dionysos

ASKLEPIEION

N

0   50   100
Yards

as the Parthenon and the Hephaisteion. The Parthenon was the crown of the Acropolis, visible from all over Athens and towering over the other buildings in the precinct (*68*).

When the visitor had climbed the steep western side, he came through the narrow rising passage of the Propylaia and saw to the left the great bronze statue of Athena Promachos (the champion), which was also a work of Pheidias, made out of the spoils of the Persians who fought at Marathon. The accounts show that it was made in the ten years or so before the Parthenon. The statue was 30 feet high, helmeted, with a spear in the right hand and the shield on the ground on the left side. On a clear day the point of the spear could be seen by sailors sailing in from Sounion. To his right the visitor to the Acropolis would see the upper part of the Parthenon, slightly askew so that he would see along the north side as well as the west front which faced him. If the modern reconstruction of the forecourt is right, he would again be forced to have a slanting view when he finally entered the gateway and saw the whole height of the temple. In spite of his elaborate arrangements to counteract the visual distortion caused by long rows of parallel columns, the architect planned for a slanting view, and similar arrangements can be seen in other Greek temples.

The visitor sees the Doric temple (*69*) with its great pedimental figures and below them the square metopes set between their triglyphs, and when he gets nearer he can see the frieze high on the walls of the shrine inside the outer row of columns. If he follows the direction of the figures on the frieze, he will look first at the west front, then go down the north side, then enter the shrine through the east door, come out again and come down the south side on his return.

The west pediment shows the contest of Athena and Poseidon for the right to be the guardian of Athens. Poseidon struck the rock with his trident and produced a spring; Athena gave them the first olive. The verdict went to Athena. The olive was an essential element in Attic life, and, as we have said, the oil of the trees descended from Athena's original olive was given as a prize in the painted amphorae at the Panathenaic games. Athena won, but Poseidon, as the god of the sea, on which Athenian naval and commercial supremacy depended, and as the god of horses, the patron of the Athenian knights, the richest and noblest youths of Athens, also had a great claim on their affections, a great and very

69   View of Parthenon

old claim, since he was the god of Nestor's Pylos, from which the Athenians drew their kings in the last stages of the Mycenaean period. On the pediment, which we know from a seventeenth-century drawing and some surviving fragments, the olive was in the middle. Poseidon started back to the right and Athena moved to the left. They make a central V, like but more explosive than the central V of the Olympia west pediment, and the lines are reversed in the rearing horses of their waiting chariots and reversed again in the figures of the two charioteers who hold in the horses. Thus the chariots, instead of making two balancing horizontal masses as in the east pediment of Olympia, are themselves worked into the echoing lines of force. Beyond the charioteers the corners are filled with minor figures and a reclining figure at the end.

The pediment is badly damaged, but the general impression of the composition is that an explosive force goes out from the central combatants and expends itself in the seated figures of the heroes and heroines of Athens and Eleusis who watch the great event, until it comes to rest in the reclining figures in the corners. All the Athenian landscape rejoices in the benefits which Athena and Poseidon confer on Athens, but attention is focused much more than at Olympia on the tremendous figures in the middle. Sophocles may have been thinking of this pediment when he wrote in his last play: 'There is a plant such as I hear not of in Asian land nor in the great Dorian island of Pelops, invincible, self-renewing, terror of enemies' spears, which flourishes most mightily in this land, the leaf of the grey olive, which nurtures our sons. Neither young nor old will sack or destroy it. For the ever-seeing eye of Zeus watches it and grey-eyed Athena. I have another great praise to tell of our mother-city, gift of the mighty god, mightiest boast of this land, fair in horses, fair in colts, fair at sea. Son of Kronos, you established her in this boast, Lord Poseidon, making for our roads first the bit which manages horses. And the oar well-rowed in skilful hands runs over the sea, following the hundred-footed Nereids.'

Beneath the pediment the metopes represented the battle of the Greeks and Amazons. The story was presumably Theseus' battle with the Amazons rather than Herakles' battle with the Amazons. These unruly women, behaving in a way which Greeks regarded as unsuitable to their sex, invaded Attica and were defeated by the

70   Parthenon: detail from west frieze, XV

disciplined forces of Theseus: Aeschylus had already alluded to the story in the *Eumenides*, and it was a subject of great paintings by Mikon in the Theseion and the Stoa Poikile. The metopes have remained on the building and are badly damaged.

On the wall of the shrine itself is the frieze with the Panathenaic procession (see above p. 86), probably the first celebration instituted by Erechtheus in the legendary past. This is the cheerful service of the Athenian people to their goddess, a service owed for the great benefits recorded in the pediment above. On the west frieze we see the young knights of the Athenian cavalry, whose patron god was Poseidon, at the start of the procession. The compositional problem must have been partly to vary the movement, partly to keep it under control. So the southernmost figure looks to the right and leads the eye round to the south side; his neighbour pulling on his boot looks towards him, so does the third figure (*70*); the fourth is having trouble with his horse which rears to the right. Only with the tenth figure does the firm leftward movement of riders start, and then it is retarded at intervals by seven more dismounted figures, the last a marshal standing at the corner.

The north frieze starts slowly with three dismounted men; then the pace quickens with men and horses overlapping. This lasts for

71 Parthenon: reconstruction of east pediment

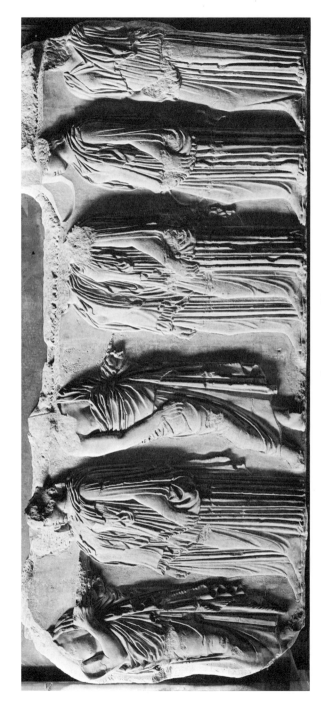

72 Parthenon: east frieze

ten of the 42 slabs. Then the horsemen thin out somewhat and are retarded by single standing figures facing right. This is followed by the horizontal groups of chariots with their horses, charioteers and attendants (here there is a reference to the race of men in armour who jumped from moving chariots; pp. 62, 86). The last ten slabs to the east end are composed of first a close-packed group of old men, who make a short quick perpendicular rhythm after the chariots (the old men in the procession carried branches of olive, Athena's special tree), then a group of musicians with lyres and flutes (perhaps in allusion to the musical competitions at the Panathenaia), then rather more widely spaced young men carrying jars of water on their shoulders and young men with trays (they were the resident aliens in red cloaks, and their trays held cakes and honeycombs), and finally the long horizontals of sheep and heifers being led to sacrifice with a youth at the end looking back down the line. The steady movement of more than 100 figures breaks down into groups alternately dominated by verticals and horizontals and is punctuated by figures looking back to the beginning.

Over the frieze the metopes on this side are badly damaged. Enough remains to show that the theme was the sack of Troy, the last ghastly night, watched by groups of gods in the three metopes at the west end and at the east end by the sun as he rises in his chariot. The will of Zeus was done, as Homer says, and it was the will of Zeus that the disciplined Greeks should conquer the immensely powerful and rich eastern power, as some 700 years later they overcame the Persians.

The visitor turns the corner to the east front, which has the door into the shrine in the centre. This pediment (71) is even more seriously damaged than the other. The centre can be reconstructed from a Roman relief, and we know from Pausanias that the theme was the birth of Athena from the head of Zeus. Zeus was seated in the centre. To the left the smith-god Hephaistos with his axe starts away (like Poseidon in the west). To the right Athena, fully armed, moves away. The rest of the pediment shows the deities receiving the tremendous news. Only the corners are left. The sun rises from the sea at the southern end; the moon sinks into the sea at the northern end. This is a bold new idea for filling the corners. Next on the left is a figure probably rightly interpreted as Herakles (73), who will carry Greek civilisation over the world as the champion

73   Herakles from east pediment of Parthenon

of Athena. Demeter is seated next him with her daughter Persephone, as the patron of the Mysteries at Eleusis, in which Herakles
was initiated. At the other end is the wonderful group of three
women which used to be called the Fates but are most probably
Hestia, Dione and Aphrodite, with astonishingly realistic drapery
that looks forward to the next generation of sculptors. For the
Athenians, birth from the head of Zeus gave their goddess a
unique claim to power and wisdom, and Hephaistos is also
highlighted as the patron of Athenian art.

The metopes below show the battle between the gods and
giants, who used their physical force to try and storm Olympos,
again a triumph of wise discipline over violence. The theme was
woven into the peplos which was given to Athena. Zeus and his
wife Hera occupy the two central metopes over the door. The
centre metopes of each half have three figures instead of two, and
the figures of the end metopes are turned inwards to hold the
whole together.

143

The frieze falls into five groups: from each end the procession approaches, a marshal beckons round the corner, then maidens carrying libation saucers, wine-jugs and incense-burners, then a bunch of marshals forming a stop. These groups are dominated by perpendiculars (*72*). Then a group of gods seated on Olympos watching the procession: they are more widely spaced and the emphasis is on the horizontals. Athena and Hephaistos are seated together at the end of the gods watching the procession from the north. Zeus and Hera are seated together at the end of the gods watching the procession from the south side. Over the door is a group of five figures: two girls with stools on their heads (they are probably the Arrhephoroi, p. 84), a priestess taking the stool from the nearer one, then a man folding a piece of cloth to give to a smaller figure. This is clearly a moment of great importance, but we have lost the clue. Is the man giving the old peplos into safe custody, and is the priestess receiving the new peplos?

Through the door the visitor entered the shrine, and at the end, filling most of the width, which is reduced by an inner circuit of columns, he saw the 40-foot ivory and gold statue of Athena, helmeted, with the aegis on her breast, her left hand resting on her shield (like the Promachos) and a golden Victory in her right hand. We only know the statue from reduced copies and can form no idea of its style, but by reading Pausanias' description we can guess what Pheidias was saying. The outside of Athena's shield had reliefs representing the battle of Greeks and Amazons, who were shown storming the Acropolis. This picked up the theme of the western metopes. The theme of the eastern metopes, the battle of the gods and giants, was picked up by the decoration of the inside of the shield. On Athena's sandals was the battle of Lapiths and Centaurs, picking up the theme of the southern metopes, which the visitor would see as he returned from the shrine. This again is the story of the triumph of Greek discipline over violence, as we have seen in discussing the west pediment of Olympia.

Thus the statue of Athena summed up the decoration of the temple. The Athenians, rooted in Attic earth and protected by a uniquely powerful and wise goddess, receive the gifts of the gods. The pious service represented by the frieze and the discipline which enabled the gods to defeat the giants and the Greeks to defeat Trojans, Amazons and Centaurs are the qualities which Periklean Athens needs in its citizens to preserve its freedom. If words are to

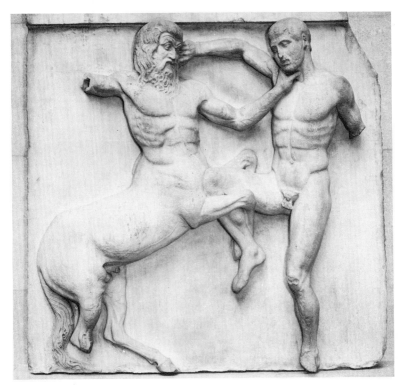

74   Parthenon: metope. Lapith and Centaur

be put into the mouth of Pheidias' Athena, they can be found in
Sophocles' *Ajax*, a play probably produced when the Parthenon
was being planned or in the early days of building; there Athena
says to Odysseus: 'Seeing these things, never yourself speak a
boastful word to the gods, nor be puffed with pride, if your hand
is heavier than another's or your coffers deeper. For in a single day
all human things may set and rise again. The gods love the modest
and hate the wicked.'

The visitor returns by the south side. He sees on the frieze the
other stream of the Panathenaic procession: the main divisions on
the frieze are the same as on the north side. Above, the metopes
represent the battle between the Lapiths and Centaurs (*74*), the
subject of the west pediment of Olympia. Here it is divided
between 32 metopes.

75   Demeter, Triptolemos, and Persephone

A marble relief from Eleusis (75) which can be dated about 440
or rather later gives us a better idea of Pheidian gods than the
copies of the Athena Parthenos. It was evidently popular, as a
copy was found in Rome and is now in New York. It is composed
as a metope: Demeter on the left and her daughter Persephone on

146

the right turn inward towards the boy Triptolemos, who is being sent out to teach agriculture to the world. This is one of the proudest claims of Athens, that a hero from Eleusis (not as the Sophists quoted by Sophocles in the *Antigone* said, 'a clever human technician') gave agriculture to the world. Here Triptolemos is without the snake-propelled chariot seen in many pictures; the emphasis is on his 'briefing' by the goddesses. The figures repeat Pheidian statues, which

76 Head of Artemis

were evidently famous, as they also are known in Roman copies. We see clearly how the drapery has changed since Olympia. Persephone wears the thin Ionic chiton and over it the himation makes elaborate folds; Demeter wears the peplos, but again it makes much richer folds than the peplos worn by the 'mourning' Athena. The beauty of a full-scale original of this time can be seen in a marble head, perhaps from a statue of Artemis, which was found in the Agora (*76*).

The classical style appears in its purest form on the Athenian white lekythoi, which were made for funeral offerings. The tall narrow shape was designed for placing on the narrow steps of the tomb, and they can be seen thus placed on several vase paintings of tombs. They contained an offering of perfumed oil to the dead, and they show the dead as they lived. Our example is by one of the best painters of these vases, whom we call the Achilles painter from a big red-figure amphora with the single picture of Achilles (*77*). A soldier says farewell to his wife as she sits in her room. This is the purest classical style and there is no trace of emotion: it is we who know that the vase was buried in a grave. Technically the picture brings us somewhere near great painting. The pink clay has been covered with a fine white slip. The outlines are done in diluted glaze which gives a golden-brown line.

Finally an example which contrasts directly the classical style with the strong style. An Attic bell-krater of about 440 by the

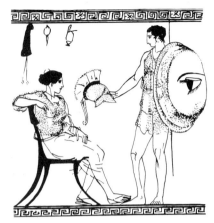

77 Woman and soldier

Lykaon painter repeats the Artemis and Aktaion story of the Pan painter (78). But all is now different. The vase has the more elegant shape of the classical period, the picture has its depth divided by rocks, there are four figures instead of two, and Aktaion is magnificently distorted as he falls backward on the rocks. The landscape, the three-quarter face, and the foreshortened right leg are now part of the competent painter's stock-in-trade. This painter has added Zeus and Lyssa (personified Madness) to the Artemis and Aktaion of the Pan painter. Zeus watches from the left, holding his flaming thunderbolt in his left hand, and Artemis stands on the right holding a torch; this makes her into a sort of fury driving Lyssa on. Lyssa wears long boots, short chiton, jacket with long sleeves, skin over the left shoulder, and hound's head over her head. The long sleeves may mean that she appeared like this on the tragic stage. The hound's head above her head is, I think, the correlative of the stag's horns and ears which appear on Aktaion's head (his hair also looks like the skin of a stag): madness enters the hounds and they think that Aktaion is a stag. The painter is telling us much more than an observer would have seen. To personify Lyssa (originally battle-lust but here hallucination as well) was not new; in poetry such mental states had long been personified, and Aeschylus had put Lyssa on the stage in the *Xantriai*, in which she drove the Maenads mad. Euripides used her later in the *Hercules Furens*, when Hera sends her to cause Herakles to mistake his wife and children for the wife and children of Eurystheus and kill them. It is a natural guess that Aeschylus also introduced Lyssa into his *Toxotides*, which dealt with the death of Aktaion. The actual scene of the rending by hounds was described in a messenger-speech. The painter has written Euaion above his picture: Euaion was the son of Aeschylus and may have acted in revivals of his father's plays after his death; was this vase possibly painted to celebrate a revival of the *Toxotides*?

78 Artemis and Aktaion

The Pan painter reduced the scene to the goddess, the hounds and the dying victim. The Lykaon painter is much more explicit; not only does he sketch in a landscape, but he uses his knowledge, as I think, of the stage production to make the whole story clear— that the hounds were driven mad, that Aktaion looked to them like a stag, that Artemis was the immediate cause and Zeus the ultimate cause. Of course, if the vase was actually painted to celebrate a stage production, he was naturally thinking of the play and wanted to introduce allusions to the play. But classical art is more explicit than early classical art even where there is an inherent contradiction between a greater realism of spatial representation and the means of explanation. This contradiction becomes even more apparent in the next period.

The Free Style: 425–370 BC

The balance achieved by the classical style did not last long. Of course, as always, some artists continued to work in the old style, but the leading artists went other ways, and indeed the Parthenon sculptures themselves show the possibility of a breakaway in two directions, formalism and realism. The long-drawn-out misery of the Peloponnesian War, which lasted with a brief gap from 431 to 403 BC, the tyranny of a small band of unscrupulous aristocrats known as the Thirty Tyrants in 403, the restoration of the democracy after a bitter civil war, the resumption of imperialist policy in the early fourth century—this chequered stretch of history is sometimes held responsible for the free style, and it is certainly the background of it, but it is more profitable to point out parallel phenomena in thought, poetry and prose than to look for an answer in political history.

The beginning of the free style is set at 425 chiefly to exclude the great classical works discussed in the preceding chapter and to include the Nike temple (79) on the Acropolis of Athens, which celebrated the peace of 421, the beginning of a breathing space in the Peloponnesian War. The end date, 370, is chosen more arbitrarily as a moment when the free style in art was no longer dominant, when Plato's Academy and Isocrates' school of rhetoric were both well established, a moment before Aristotle joined the Academy and before the power of Macedon had made itself felt.

The two great masters of tragedy, Sophocles and Euripides, went on writing until nearly the end of the fifth century: Euripides died in 407; Sophocles died early in 405. Sophocles' last three surviving plays belong to this period: the *Electra*, the *Philoctetes* and the *Oedipus Coloneus*. We know far too little about Sophocles to draw a convincing picture of his development. In all the four earlier plays the chorus sing their first very impressive song by themselves in the orchestra; in all the three late plays their first song is a lyric dialogue with an actor taking a considerable part. To this extent the clear contrast between spoken iambic trimeters and sung lyrics of the chorus gives place to a more varied texture, and occasionally at emotional high-points the spoken iambics of an actor give place to other metres. Euripides had used the lyric dialogue form for the parodos earlier, but in this period he also varies the texture by introducing considerable dialogue scenes in recitative trochaic tetrameters and long lyric monodies for actors, while his spoken iambics themselves have a shimmering rhythm which makes them much less stately than before.

This blurring of the clear lines and contrasts of classical tragedy is, of course, only the outward sign of an inner change. Sophocles does not abandon the divine framework of his plays: in each of the late plays an oracle is announced in the prologue and the play ends with its fulfilment, but within this framework enormous emphasis is placed on the chief character and on the range and depth of

79 Nike temple

emotions through which the chief character is made to pass: in the last three plays the secondary characters count for far less, the chief character counts for far more, the story is a story of suffering rather than of doing, and the chief character is presented from the beginning as warped by some terrible experience.

In the *Philoctetes* the use of this formula nearly breaks the framework because Neoptolemos finally agrees to sail home with Philoktetes and forget about Troy; but the story says that Philoktetes went to Troy, and Sophocles introduces Herakles, who descends from heaven and persuades Philoktetes to go to Troy. This is a quite unusual use of the *deus ex machina*: here Philoktetes has achieved exactly what he wants, and Sophocles only saves the story by introducing the one person who could persuade Philoktetes, Herakles, whose miraculous bow he possesses. A warped character cannot change direction without a major psychological disturbance, a conversion or a vision or the like: in stage terms this is rendered by the appearance of Herakles as *deus ex machina*.

The obvious new elements in these plays are an interest in abnormal psychology and the display of this by the great range of emotion through which the chief character passes and passes quickly from the depths of despair to the height of joy. This agonising see-saw of emotion is peculiarly Sophoclean, and the whole play is directed to portraying it. Euripides rather shows the effect of a disastrous event on the whole family concerned in it, including the slaves of the family, and every member of the family influences the action. But for the depths there are many Euripidean parallels: Kreousa's monody in the *Ion* or Andromache's misery in the *Trojan Women*, when she hears that her baby Astyanax is to be killed. Euripides also has single scenes showing abnormal psychology: Orestes at the beginning of his name-play, Pentheus and Agave in the *Bacchae*. And twice Euripides allows a character in the depth of misery to smash the whole framework within which the play up to that point has apparently been proceeding.

In 415 Euripides reverted to Aeschylean practice and wrote a trilogy of three connected plays. In the *Alexandros* (of which considerable papyrus fragments survive) the young Paris, who has been exposed and brought up by shepherds, defeats the Trojan princes at the games; Hekabe and Deiphobos against Hektor's advice try to kill him; he is recognised at the last moment and accepted into Priam's household in spite of Kassandra's gloomy prophecies; a god (probably Apollo) foretells his marriage with Helen. In the second play, the *Palamedes*, the hero Palamedes is falsely accused of treachery by Odysseus and put to death by Agamemnon, while his brother prophesies destruction to the Greek fleet. The *Trojan Women*, which is preserved complete, is composed of scenes from the sack of Troy, Kassandra wildly prophesying that her marriage to Agamemnon will bring him death, Andromache torn from her baby Astyanax, Hekabe confronting Helen and begging Menelaos to kill her, Hekabe lamenting the dead body of Astyanax. My point here is not that Euripides is still using the principle of variation—recognition-play, camp-play, play about ill-treated women—nor that he has used the trilogy form brilliantly: the *Trojan Women* gains enormously if we remember, when we see Kassandra prophesying Agamemnon's doom, that she had prophesied only too truly the doom of Troy in the first play, that Odysseus' useless murder of the infant Astyanax is all of a piece with his judicial murder of Palamedes in the second play, and that the confrontation of Helen and Hekabe is the logical conclusion to the rescue of Paris and the prophecy of the rape of Helen in the first play. My point is rather this: Euripides has apparently accepted the myth of the Judgment of Paris, and the whole trilogy has proceeded on that assumption; when Helen defends herself, she says that Hekabe was responsible for the Trojan War because she gave birth to Paris, Paris judged the goddesses and Aphrodite gave him Helen as a bride. Hekabe answers (969 ff.): 'I don't believe the goddesses had a beauty competition. Don't make them fools to doll up your own vice. My son was outstandingly beautiful. Your mind seeing him was turned into Aphrodite. You saw his foreign clothes and his gold, and you went mad. Menelaos' house was not big enough for your extravagant desires.' In other words this is a human story of the small-town girl who falls for the rich and attractive foreigner. But this interpretation makes nonsense of the whole trilogy.

The other instance is equally startling. In the *Hercules Furens* the play proceeds on the assumption that Herakles is serving Eurystheus because Hera has commanded it and that he is the son of Zeus. When Herakles has killed Lykos, personified madness (Lyssa, whom we discussed in connection with the Aktaion story) enters, sent by Hera to drive Herakles mad so that he will kill his own wife and children. At the end of the play Herakles, returning to sanity, sits pondering suicide, when his friend Theseus arrives to try and comfort him. 'Why should I live? Let Zeus' noble wife dance till Olympos shakes with the beat of her feet. She has achieved her wish by utterly destroying the best man in Greece.' Theseus tries to comfort him with the thought that not even the gods escape crime but they go on living on Olympos; therefore a mere mortal must bear his fate. Herakles answers (1340): 'I have never believed that the gods commit crimes nor that one god can be the master of another god. If god is truly god, he needs nothing. These are the unfortunate figments of poets.' But if this is true, it makes nonsense of the whole play up to now, which has assumed that Herakles is the son of Zeus and has performed his labours and ultimately been driven mad by the jealousy of Hera. It seems that Euripides occasionally gives his characters at a moment of deepest suffering an insight into a world quite different from the world in which they have existed up till then. They desert a world in which gods behave like unprincipled men and play with men and women as their toys, for a world in which god is detached and absolute, and man is controlled by his own emotions or controls them. This may be Euripides' own view, but he only allows it to appear at rare moments.

It is fair to say that in these late plays both dramatists emphasise human passions and emotions and sufferings, all that is covered by the Greek word pathos. At the same time Thucydides was writing his history of the Peloponnesian War, in which he explained historical events in terms of what we should nowadays call basic human drives such as fear and greed. Much of his terminology and particularly the habit of expressing these drives as a neuter adjective with a definite article 'the daring' or 'the fearful' or 'the prudent', comes from the doctors, who used this terminology because they thought of 'the intelligent' or 'the fierce' or 'the cowardly' as a physical constituent of the brain in just the same way as they thought of 'the hot', 'the cold', 'the wet' and 'the dry' as physical constituents of the body.

This whole kind of analysis has several results, some of which concern us. One is the interest in emotion and suffering (both covered by the Greek word pathos) in its various forms, which I have illustrated from tragedy and which can also be illustrated in art. A second is the possibility of personifying these terms so as to talk about them and represent them: for these purposes feminine abstracts can be thought of as goddesses. We have already seen that Lyssa, 'madness', can appear on the stage and can be represented in art. Now the range is greatly extended, and one of the doctors writes: 'Medicine has discovered constraints by which Nature may be forced without harm to herself to make discharges.' The words suggest one woman interrogating another, and the scene could be so represented. To express it thus is a convenient and impressive way of saying that all doctors trained in experimental technique can use the technique on all sick bodies (Nature) without doing them harm.

The third result, or perhaps one should rather say that it is a parallel phenomenon, is the exploitation of psychology by rhetoric. If a man can be spoken of as a sum of such psychological parts, he becomes a creature of predictable reactions. A speech can be so designed as to arouse the required reactions in a jury or in a legislative assembly, and one means of doing this is to present a client as a man psychologically incapable of performing the action ascribed to him by his opponent. This is the period of the first great rhetoricians, in theory and in practice: Gorgias came to Athens in 427 and Thrasymachosis mentioned in the same year; Antiphon's speech on the murder of Herodes has been dated 424. The influence of rhetoric on tragedy and on Thucydides is extremely clear.

Curiously enough psychological argument and emotional perorations do not exclude extreme formalism as another means of moving an audience. Where Thrasymachos was famous for his pathetic perorations, Gorgias was famous for his antitheses, for his parallel clauses sometimes with rhyming endings, and apparently these means were as effective in winning an audience as psychological or emotional realism.

In verse also the Greeks showed the same delight in formalism. In Euripides' *Bacchae*, just after Pentheus has expressed his scorn for the aged Kadmos and Teiresias, who propose to take part in the rites of the new god Dionysos, and has sent his guards to hunt down the leader of the new religion, the chorus of Maenads, the devotees of Dionysos, pray to 'Holiness, queen of gods', to listen to the sacrilegious madness of Pentheus. Then they pray that they may be transported to Cyprus, where Aphrodite and the Erotes dwell or to Olympos where the Muses live. This can be called an escape chorus, because the type is known from other plays: at a bad moment in the action the chorus pray that a god may remove them somewhere else. Here the verse has very pretty short echoing lines of aeolic metre (409 f.): 'and where the beautiful Pierian seat of the Muses is, the solemn slope of Olympos, thither lead me, Bromios, Bromios, leader of bacchants, god of our song. There are the Graces, there is Desire, there the Bacchants may hold their revel.'

Such a chorus immediately brings to mind the vases of the so-called rich style, painted by the Meidias painter and his contemporaries at the end of the fifth century and the beginning of the fourth. The analogy lies partly in the style of choruses of this kind, the pretty echoes of the short lines, the coincidence of words and metre, the colourful adjectives, partly also, in this particular case, in the subject-matter. Euripides transports us into a fantasy world where Aphrodite, Erotes, Muses, Graces, Desire, and (in the next verse) Dionysos and Eirene (Peace) dwell among the devotees of Dionysos. The Meidias painter and his colleagues show just

80 Aphrodite, Chrysippos, and Pompe

such an intermingling of figures connected with Aphrodite and figures connected with Dionysos. When they paint Dionysos among his Maenads they sometimes give them names: Peace, Brightness, Good Cheer, or even Tragedy or Comedy. So this fantasy world links up with the psychological analysis discussed above: such a picture can be interpreted as meaning that Good Cheer or the poetic creation of drama are dependent on the ecstasy which is personified as Dionysos.

One of the Meidias painter's school painted a very pretty little lekythos (80), a lady's scent-bottle of the squat, stable form which is common now, with very beautiful formalised floral orna-

81   Rape of the Leukippidai

ment under the handle. Aphrodite is seated and a small Eros points
to her as he moves up to a young man called Chrysippos; beyond
Chrysippos is a seated women labelled Pompe. The painter is
telling a story which we know well from later comedy: a young
man fell in love with a girl when she was taking part in a religious
procession. Instead of illustrating the moment he puts the young
man between the personification of the Procession (Pompe) and
Eros, while Aphrodite diverts her attention from her worshipper
on the left to look benevolently in his direction. If the vase is a
present from the young man, the girl will read in it the story of
their first meeting.

One of the most perfectly finished vases by the Meidias painter
himself is a hydria which is signed by Meidias as potter and gives
the painter his name. The shape of this water-pot is very elegant
with twisted sidehandles, elaborate mouth and foot, magnificent
floral ornament under the pouring handle at the back, bands of
ornament framing the two figure-scenes on the front, which divide
the flowing shape into separate areas, as it might be a pediment

and a frieze. The lower picture is a simple frieze with Herakles seated in the garden of the Hesperides while a nymph picks him a golden apple from the tree guarded by a snake; this we have already discussed (see above p. 110). The larger picture on the Meidias painter's hydria (*81*) is skilfully adapted to the space with a strong vertical made by the image of the goddess, the group of Kastor and one of the daughters, and the altar, and with balancing horizontals of the two chariots above and the fleeing women below. The story is the rape of the two daughters of Leukippos by Kastor and Polydeukes.

An interesting point is the stylisation of the image in the shrine from which the girls are carried off, as a primitive idol. We have noticed a similar archaistic idol on the rather later Iphigeneia vase (p. 92). I add three other notable instances of late fifth-century archaism. The sculptor Alkamenes, who was a pupil of Pheidias working in the last quarter of the fifth century, made a Herm, a pillar surmounted by the head of Hermes, for the Propylaia, the great entrance-way to the Acropolis. The head is not the youthful head of the young god, which is normal at this time, but a bearded head with corkscrew curls in the fashion of the late sixth century. Secondly, the special amphorae made for prizes in the Panathenaic games now have on one side an Athena painted in the style of the late sixth century, somewhat exaggerated, and on the other, athletes in contemporary style. Thirdly, a jug of a special shape, which was probably again a special form devised for some ritual connected with the Panathenaia, has a young Hermes with a cloak that falls in elaborate swallow-tail folds reminiscent of the late archaic period, but the floral ornament under the handles includes a foreshortened and shaded bell-flower in the most modern style (*82*). Therefore, though from one point of view the archaistic style might be regarded as the logical extreme of the rich formal style, in fact it is not yet a style in the normal sense but a manner with a very restricted application.

At the end of Aristophanes' *Knights*, which was produced in 424, the scruffy, toothless, irritable old Demos,

82 Hermes

the personification of the Athenian people, is 'rejuvenated' so that he appears 'bright in his old-fashioned dress', 'as he was when he dined with Aristides and Miltiades'. The desire for the good old times takes visible shape in the dress of the Persian War period as worn by the victors of Marathon and Salamis. So the archaistic figures of Athena and Hermes and the archaistic images of other

83 Aphrodite

84 Caryatid from
Erechtheion

gods may be meant to recall the sanctity of the good old times before the Sophists, the philosophers and the doctors undermined the traditional religion. It is an acknowledgment that traditional forms of religion have their own peculiar value; and for the first time, perhaps, in high poetry this value is reasserted at the end of the chorus of the *Bacchae* quoted above (430): 'The beliefs and uses of the common herd, those I would accept.'

The rich style can also be found in sculpture. Very near to the seated Aphrodite of the Meidias' painter is an over-lifesize marble statue from the Agora, which has been interpreted as Aphrodite(*83*). The goddess steps forward with her weight on the left leg. She wears a long thin chiton with deeply cut, narrow folds over her feet and an elaborate curving system over her body. Her heavier himation is round her waist and over her left arm with realistic, deeply cut folds. This is the style of the Parthenon 'Fates' carried to a further stage of elaboration, and it has been suggested that the sculptor was one of the sculptors who worked on the balustrade of the temple of Nike.

The main surviving sculpture of two new buildings on the Acropolis, the Caryatids of the Erechtheion and the balustrade of the Nike temple, shows a startling difference in style, although they both were probably built between 420 and 410. The Erechtheion is a strangely untidy building because it has to unite the various venerable old shrines in one building. It has a remarkable north porch with the entablature supported by six marble female figures (*84*). These Caryatids look rather as if they had walked off the east frieze of the Parthenon, and perhaps they are meant to recall the solemn women of the Panathenaic procession. It is true that the folds of the peplos over the stiff leg and on the overfall, where it swings across over the higher hip, are more elaborate than on any earlier peplos figure, but they carry on the classical tradition of sculpture.

The little temple of Athena Nike (Victory) was built to celebrate the Peace at the end of the first ten years of the Peloponnesian War. It stands out on the bastion of rock on the right as one ascends the Acropolis towards the Propylaia, and even now, when it has lost its roof and the akroteria at each end, which would have completed its shape, it is a marvel of delicacy and grace (79). Soon after its completion the bastion on which it stood was edged by a balustrade or parapet the outside of which was sculptured. The sculpture was on the three sides of the parapet, the north side slanting off the way up the Acropolis, the west side, and the south side: a short returning wall from the north side showed four Nikai proceeding towards the temple. Each of the three long walls had

the same general composition: in the centre Nikai bringing bulls to sacrifice at an altar of Athena; at the outsides attendant Nikai and seated Athenas punctuated by trophies (tree-trunks adorned or being adorned with armour). There were originally 50 figures; probably there was one Athena on each side and all the rest were winged Victories. The subject-matter is extraordinarily jejune and the composition forms itself into roughly symmetrical groups. The work was, however, famous and inspired some direct copies and many imitations. These show how boring exact repetition can become unless the intention is a purely formal frieze. Here, however, every figure was slightly different so

85 Nike balustrade: sandal-binder

161

that the whole frieze becomes a series of variations on an essentially simple theme. The stylistic differences suggest that six masters were employed and that each made half one of the long sides. The Nike binding her sandal ends the west flank of the south side (*85*). Even without its head, which was probably turned to look at the spectator, the figure is tremendously effective with the great curved wings echoing the system of folds set up between the legs and repeating the curve of the body as the Nike bends forward, and she is at the same time anchored by the tiny repetitive verticals of the chiton-folds on either side of her standing leg. Another slab gives two Nikai on either side of the bull which is being brought to sacrifice in the centre of the north side. The strong movement to the right of the profile Nike, of the long slanting bull's body and of the frontal Nike (her frontality makes her seem to move more slowly) is checked and reversed by two standing Nikai in the next slab with the sacrificial altar between them. The very rich drapery and small crinkly folds of the Nike on the left of the bull is quite different from the bold linear systems of the himation and peplos of the Nike in front of the bull, and for this reason they have been attributed to different sculptors; the second sculptor, particularly if, as is probable, he also made the standing Nike of the next slab, is much nearer to the Caryatids from the Erechtheion. The distance between the classical style at its most elaborate and the rich style is in fact not great. This variety of styles and variety of detailed poses makes the Nike parapet, in its present fragmentary condition and without the glory of its original colour and in spite of its repetitive subject, a work of very great charm.

The grave-relief of Hegeso shows the rich style applied to funeral monuments (*86*). The new form of marble grave-relief comes in about 440 and continues to about 317 when the sumptuary laws of Demetrios of Phaleron put an end to this type of monument. The figures are enclosed in a framework of pilasters, architrave, and pediment with akroteria, like a small shrine. The akroteria at least, if not also the pediment, were always ornamented with painted designs and the background would be filled in with solid colour. Sometimes it is difficult to decide who has died, and probably once the relief was set up in the burial ground of the Kerameikos other members of the family would be buried beneath it. Here there is no doubt that Hegeso is the dead woman

86 Grave-relief: Hegeso

87 Grave-relief: comic poet

and she is shown in her house with her maid. The difference between her and the woman on the Achilles painter's lekythos is the difference between the classical style and the style of the Nike parapet, with its rich folds at the waist and round the feet, and the use of the folds to model the maid's body and legs. Hegeso is choosing a necklace out of her jewel box; presumably the necklace was added in paint. As on the lekythos, the dead woman is represented as she was in life.

The Hegeso relief is a very good specimen of the numerous grave-reliefs of this time, which, whether in the rich style or in a continuation of the classical style, continue the spirit of the white lekythoi of the Parthenon period. Rarely a figure on a relief shows emotion. At first glance a relief now in Lyme Park, Stockport (87), seems to belong to the same class as Hegeso; the dead represented as they were in life. A comic poet is seated with a roll of papyrus in his left hand (the roll is broken off level with the top of his hand and therefore does not appear in the photograph). He holds the mask of a comic slave in his right hand, and the mask of an old man hangs on the wall in the background. If we like to think of him as Aristophanes writing his last play, the date would fit and the size of the grave-relief suggests a famous poet. For us, at any rate, it is the earliest of the illustrations of dramatic poets composing a speech, mask in hand. But in this relief the contrast between life and death is not something which we supply but it is built into the relief itself. The deep disillusionment and sorrow of the poet's head with the furrows on either side of the nose and the close clipped beard contrasts with the gay shamelessness of the slave mask.

We have more evidence for realism of emotion and realism in representing the third dimension in painting than in sculpture.

This emphasis on emotion corresponds to the emotional scenes of drama and the pathetic perorations of law-court speeches. In big painting Zeuxis painted a picture of Menelaos standing by the tomb of Agamemnon, drenched in tears—a complete rejection of classical restraint. Was it perhaps this picture that made Aristotle contrast him with Polygnotos and say that his painting had no ethos, no moral colouring? Parrhasios, the Ephesian artist who claimed that he had reached the boundaries of his art, was famous for representing the subtleties of expression. It is this skill that is brought out in the conversation between him and Sokrates, which is reported by Xenophon: Sokrates, after pointing out that the painter can represent concave and convex, light and dark, etc. (spatial realism of which more will be said later), and that he can paint an ideal by combining beautiful parts from many different people (this is a clear allusion to Zeuxis' painting of Helen, for which the people of Kroton provided him with five models so that he could combine the most beautiful parts of each), asks Parrhasios whether he can paint the characteristics of the soul; he at first denies the possibility and then admits that these things can be represented in the faces: magnificence and freedom, humility and servility, prudence and wisdom, pride and vulgarity. And when he painted the Athenian Demos, possibly as a double-sided mask of an old man, he was able to show it as angry, unjust, fickle, and at the same time merciful and open to entreaty, as boastful and servile, as fierce and cowardly. These two artists, like Euripides, seem to have been at home at both extremes of the free style: Zeuxis painted a rose-wreathed Eros but also a tear-drenched Menelaos; Parrhasios painted a rose-fed Theseus but also a tortured Prometheus.

A group of white lekythoi from the end of the century show something of this emotional style. There is nothing new in putting the tomb in the picture, but in the time of the Achilles painter, if the tomb was represented, the dead man stood unmoved beside it and a woman, equally unmoved, put offerings on the steps. Now deep grief is expressed in postures and in expression. A lekythos of this group, which is called Group R, shows the young man seated on his tomb with sad eyes, drooping mouth and untidy hair, and a man and a woman standing by (*88*). The restraint of classical lekythoi has vanished; grief is unashamedly expressed. Apart from this complete change of aim, which accounts for the extremely

88 Funeral scene: Attic white-
lekythos

expressive features (notice particularly the treatment of the
boy's eyes and lips), the lekythoi of this group show a new
and daring treatment of outline, on this vase particularly
the right forearm and left leg of
the seated figure recall Pliny's
statement that Parrhasios 'won
the palm in outlines': the Hellenistic critics quoted by Pliny
praised him for outlines 'which
promised more behind them
and showed even what they
hid'. This is a difficult way of
saying that Parrhasios did his
modelling by his outlines, and
something of that can be seen
on the lekythos.

A contemporary white lekythos (*89*) by another painter
shows a youth seated on a low
mound in front of a grave stele:
two friends visit him from either
side. This painter uses more
colour and more variety of
colour than the other; the folds
of the youth's white himation
are done in lines of dark brown;
the young man's body is modelled in flesh colour with darker
brown shading. The stele behind has a blue palmette on a
dark violet ground framed at
the bottom by violet acanthus
leaves. Here we can see something of the palette and some-
thing of the technique of Zeuxis, whom Quintilian credits with
discovering the system of light and shade. Lucian praises Zeuxis'
skill in the mixture and juxtaposition of colour, and he painted

grapes on scenery so successfully that the birds came and pecked them.

It looks as if the Hellenistic critics drew a distinction between Parrhasios, who used outline to suggest a third dimension, and Zeuxis, who used colour and shading to represent a third dimension. Zeuxis may have been painting in Athens before 425, and he was certainly painting in Macedon in the last decade of the fifth century. He was the pupil of Apollodoros of Athens, whom Pliny dates rather too late in 410. Pliny says Apollodoros was the first man to portray species, 'appearances', i.e. the momentary appearance of a scene or figure instead of its more permanent character. He was called skiagraphos, the painter who used shading, and he wrote on his works 'Easier to criticise than to imitate'. He was therefore conscious of himself as a revolutionary. For us, who have lost all ancient painting, the revolution is still apparent when we compare the shaded coloured surfaces of the late lekythos with the flat coloured surfaces on the Achilles painter's lekythos.

The ancient lexikon says that Apollodoros was called skiagraphos instead of skenographos, implying that he had a predecessor who was called skenographos. There can be little doubt that this was Agatharchos of Samos. Agatharchos, Apollodoros, Zeuxis and Parrhasios were a quartet of overlapping contemporaries who tackled the problem of representing the third dimension in different ways—perspective, shading, and suggestive outline.

Vitruvius implies that the use of perspective began with the scenery painted by Agatharchos. Foreshortening for particular objects such as shields or chariot-wheels or chairs can be traced back to Polygnotos and even before. But Agatharchos, however ineffectively in

89 Funeral scene: Attic white-lekythos

167

90   Return of a reveller

practice, was trying to organise space on a larger scale with his foreshortened buildings. It is tempting to connect his scenery with the rebuilding of the theatre of Dionysos some time about 430 (p. 91). What the audience saw was a stage surmounted by a central door, which stood out from a long wall divided by columns or pilasters in panels. It was these panels which carried Agatharchos' pictures of perspective buildings when a tragedy needing a palace or temple scene was performed.

On a small scale the painter of an Attic wine-jug has shown his interest in these problems (90). The extremely satisfying shape was common in this period and had special connections with the Anthesteria, the spring festival of Dionysos (p. 79). The wreathed stalwart is certainly returning from a party with his lyre; whether the woman, who comes with a lamp to answer his knock on the door, is his wife or whether he is proposing to make a night of it, is perhaps uncertain. Her gesture, fingers to chin, shows that she foresees a rough night. The artist wants to make clear that she is inside the house and the reveller outside, and he has used some of the new tricks to show it. Another painter, who was working about 375, made a determined attempt to get depth into the drinking party with which he decorated a kalyx-krater. In the background the two white columns probably mark the doorway of the men's dining room into the courtyard; in front of them is a couch with a white cushion, on which four revellers, two bearded and two unbearded, recline; in front of them a white girl dressed in white playing the flute; and in the foreground a couch with two banqueters; the front couch is covered with a white cloth, so that the sequence of white leads the eye into the depth.

Even with our modest sources we can appreciate the two great innovations in the art of the late fifth and early fourth century, emotionalism and realism, which won them the condemnation of Plato. Plato was born in 427, and the art which we have been describing was the art of his childhood, youth and middle age. His Sokrates, like Xenophon's, knew about Zeuxis' ideal Helen, and he knew the technical terms like skiagraphia. His account in the third book of the *Republic* of the healthy place for the young guardians may have been inspired by some picture of the garden of the Hesperides, but the art which the young guardians were to be allowed to see was to be carefully censored, and excluded 'this immoral, undisciplined, servile, and misformed element'. 'This' here means 'which we see in contemporary art.' The great attack is developed in the tenth book of the *Republic*, which was probably written between 384 and 370. It is primarily an attack on tragedy, and particularly Euripidean tragedy, as corrupting the youth by encouraging them to identify themselves with the unworthy and over-emotional figures of the tragic stage. Painting is brought in as a parallel art, on which Plato can make his first point that the representation (in the picture or on the stage) is inferior to its original and still more inferior to the philosopher's universal. The object which he chooses for this demonstration is a kline. Kline is the word for the couch on which drinkers recline at the symposion. The couch in the painting is only a copy of the couch made by the carpenter, which is itself only a copy of the Idea of a couch. The painter only reproduces a single aspect of a carpenter's couch; he only creates an illusion, which deceives children and madmen. Similarly the tragic poet knows nothing of what he represents, but he carries off his ignorance by the colours of rhythm and music. Anyone who comes to the painter's flat surface with a measuring rod will show that his projections and recessions do not exist; therefore the painter does not appeal to the reason but to the emotions. Similarly the tragic poet does not represent the actions which proceed from reason (the reasonable man is silent and displays no emotion) but the actions which proceed from emotion: Plato is thinking perhaps of Euripidean scenes like Orestes seeing the Furies, or Agave holding the head of Pentheus. 'The dramatic poet may rightly be called the complement of the painter. He is like him in that his creations bear little relation to the truth, and in the fact that he is concerned with a part of the soul which is not the best.'

He obviously could have gone on to show that Zeuxis and Parrhasios produced emotional painting, just as Euripides produced emotional scenes in tragedy, but painting is not the main object of his attack so that he does not need to cover this ground too. For his purpose, which is to show that the parallel art fails to add to knowledge but does appeal to the emotions rather than reason, the couch painted in perspective provides the perfect example. The great perspective-painter in Athens was Agatharchos, and it was presumably the dining room (andron) of Alkibiades' house that he decorated. He may have peopled the walls with revellers on perspective couches to give an illusionistic extension of the actual banquet. Did Plato visit this house as a child and never forget his disillusionment when the wall proved to be flat?

This is a harmless guess. What is more important is the violence of Plato's reaction to emotional and realistic tragedy and painting. We have seen such criticisms of realistic films in the twenties and of realistic television since the Second World War. We may wonder whether Plato or his modern successors allow enough for the toughness of the young mind or are wise in trying to give it too pure a food. That the attack had only a little effect can be seen in the art of the next generation.

The Late Classical Style: 370–325 BC

A convenient bottom limit is the year 325, shortly before Alexander and Aristotle died and Menander produced his first play. With the successors of Alexander, Ptolemy in Egypt, Antipater in Macedon, Antigonos, Seleukos and Lysimachos in the islands, Asia and north-eastern Europe, the Hellenistic age is fairly started, and the New Comedy of Menander, his contemporaries and successors, was the new literary form which spread over the greater Greek world and was rapidly adopted by Rome. Viewed from today the middle quarters of the fourth century look like a period of preparation for the explosion of Greek civilisation over the inhabited world which followed the conquests of Alexander. In Athens from about 360 the obvious prospect was the growth of Philip of Macedon, whom some, like Demosthenes, regarded as a semi-barbarian tyrant bent on the destruction of Greek freedom, but others, like Isokrates, welcomed as a champion who would lead the Greeks against their ancient enemies the Persians. Neither party made an accurate appreciation. The anti-Macedonians underrated Macedonian culture, forgetting that the tragic poet Euripides and the painter Zeuxis had both been invited to the Macedonian court in the late fifth century, and therefore did not foresee how much consideration Old Greece would receive from the new rulers. The pro-Macedonians naturally could not foresee either the staggering genius of Alexander or the powerful personalities of his successors, and they viewed the future purely in terms of military conquest and not of the spread of Greek civilisation.

But in fact the careful political theorising of Plato and Aristotle with its practical experiments, sometimes disastrous as in Syracuse, sometimes successful as with Hermias of Atarnae, bore considerable fruit in the organisation and social life of the Hellenistic kingdoms, and in the relations of the Greek cities with each other. The fruits were very various. It is difficult to tell how much Alexander's policy was influenced by his association with Aristotle in his youth, but certainly the sumptuary and educational policy of Demetrios of Phaleron in Athens in the late fourth century was a direct reflection of Aristotelian and Platonic political thought, and he took with him to Alexandria the whole idea of scholarship, to be copied in due course at Pergamon. We can also see the reflection of fourth-century social and political thinking in the arrangements between Hellenistic Greek cities to restore each others' citizens when they appeared on the slave-market through capture in war, and in a much more humane treatment of slaves generally.

The two main contributions of the fourth century to the Hellenistic age may be phrased as practical humanism and scholarship. The two seem far apart from each other, and both seem remote from the uncompromising idealism of Plato's *Republic*. Yet the *Republic* contains a theoretical account of the degeneration of constitutions from philosopher-kingship to tyranny which was in later Platonic dialogues slightly remodelled to form a historical sequence. This remodelling brought with it a respect for early Athenian democracy (the democracy of the Persian War period and before), which appears also in rather different forms in the speeches of Demosthenes and Isokrates. We have noted this respect for the past already in the late fifth century, most clearly in the rejuvenation of Demos at the end of Aristophanes' *Knights*, but now the early Athenian democracy is seen as a political system which embodied certain ethical and educational ideas; on the one hand this leads to what I have called practical humanism, on the other hand a respect for the past implies a new desire for knowledge about the past, and the past included poets and artists as well as politicians and soldiers, so that scholarship can be seen as springing from the same root as practical humanism. This is, of course, an over-simplification of a complicated development, which, in so far as it affects the arts, and particularly the visual arts, we have to try and trace.

This complicated development can be seen in literature, particularly in the public and private speeches of the orators, in tragedy and comedy, as far as the remaining fragments allow us to know them, and in painting and sculpture as well as in literary and artistic theory. It is easiest to sketch the theory first before going into greater detail about the sculpture and painting, which is our chief concern. The essential stages are Plato's *Republic* and the rather earlier *Gorgias*, Plato's *Phaedrus*, written between 359 and 353, and Aristotle's *Poetics*, composed in its original form before Aristotle left Athens in 347 but enlarged and unessentially modified when he was back in Athens from 335 to 323. The *Republic* roundly condemns tragedy, comedy, and painting as feeble copies of actions and things in the transitory world of appearance and as appealing to the emotions rather than to the intellect. The *Gorgias* (502a) similarly maintains that tragedy is a form of rhetoric addressed to a crowd, and that rhetoric is not an art but a flattery, like cooking and cosmetics—its object is simply to make what is unattractive attractive.

Most surprisingly, however, in the *Gorgias* (503e) painting is not put, like tragedy and rhetoric, among the flatteries but among the arts (in the special Greek sense of techne, which includes architecture and medicine): the painter is equated with the architect and the shipbuilder; all these arts make an arrangement (taxis), in which the parts must be suited to each other so that the result is an orderly and systematic composition. The criterion of judgment is entirely different from the criteria used in the *Republic*, and probably the word taxis gives us the clue to what painting Plato means. Composition, as we shall see, was the strong point of

Sikyonian painting. This is the new clean, strong style which Plato completely forgets in the *Republic*, because the skenographia (perspective) of Agatharchos and the skiagraphia (shading) of Apollodoros and Zeuxis suits his point better.

In the *Gorgias* composition is the mark of an art, and rhetoric and tragedy are mere flatteries. In the *Phaedrus* (264c) 'every discourse ought to be composed to have, like a zoion, its own body, so as to be neither headless nor footless, but to have a middle and ends, which are so written as to suit each other and the whole'. This description of rhetoric is very close to the description of painting in the *Gorgias*, and it is certainly possible that zoion should be translated 'painted figure' rather than 'living thing'. It follows that rhetoric is now regarded as an art, and this new rhetoric also includes tragedy. In the same passage Sokrates asks (268c) what Sophocles and Euripides would say if someone told them that he knew all the tricks of making emotional speeches and thought that he could teach his pupils to write tragedy by handing on these tricks. Phaidros answers that Sophocles and Euripides would laugh out of court anyone who thought tragedy was anything else but the composition of these elements in such a way that they agree with each other and the whole; but these elements themselves are the prerequisites of tragedy, *not* tragedy. So that tragedy also has become an art in virtue of being a harmonious composition.

The date at which this momentous change in Plato's theory of rhetoric took place (and it is of course rhetoric rather than tragedy or painting with which Plato is primarily concerned in the *Phaedrus*) would seem to be between 359, when Aristotle proved in the *Grylus* that rhetoric was not an art, and 353, the bottom date for the *Phaedrus*. The next stage is Aristotle's *Poetics* (in its original form), in which the idea of organic composition plays a most important part and the 'prerequisites of tragedy' are what Aristotle calls dianoia. This original form of the *Poetics* antedates Aristotle's departure from Athens in 347, and in the same period he was also lecturing on rhetoric in Plato's Academy.

But what caused the change? We shall have to consider later how far painting and sculpture themselves changed. Probably several different factors were operating. One may have been the practical needs of the Academy itself; it is possible that without instruction in rhetoric Plato's students could not meet the necessities of public life, and therefore he had to introduce rhetoric into the curriculum.

Another factor was a change in Plato's own outlook: Plato in the later dialogues has moved nearer the real world. He is interested in history, as we have observed, and he is interested in classification, including scientific classification. Whether he himself worked on poetic theory may be doubted, but the basic form of Aristotle's *Poetics* is like that of Plato's later dialogues (*Politicus* or *Sophist*) and proceeds from a general classification of arts of imitation to a definition of tragedy, from which he deduces the rules for good tragedy.

A third factor was Aristotle's own essentially different outlook. In general Aristotle was a scientist: he was interested in what existed and wanted to know how it worked and how it came to be what it was. Tragedy and democracy might, according to Plato, be far from ideal, but they certainly existed and worked. Therefore they were for Aristotle proper subjects of inquiry.

The brief references to the historical development of poetry and art in the *Poetics* are of great interest because they point the way to the historical scholarship of the Hellenistic period. Aristotle's history of poetry may be reduced to the following scheme: (1) the giant Homer who was the ancestor of both tragedy and comedy, (2) the little men who wrote 'praises' and 'abuse' (among the latter he certainly thinks of Archilochos), (3) drama divided into (*a*) tragedy, which was first written by those who formerly wrote 'praises' and subdivides into Old Tragedy with the emphasis on ethos (here something like 'moral purpose') and New Tragedy without moral purpose but with rhetoric, (*b*) comedy, which was first written by those who formerly wrote 'abuse', and subdivides into Old Comedy with personal abuse and later Comedy with general plots. There are some signs that he thought of a parallel history of art: Polygnotos, the great painter of the strong style, is expressly equated with Sophocles, and Zeuxis, one of the great painters of the free style, with New Tragedy. Probably also he equated the caricaturist Pauson with Old Comedy. The details were left to the Hellenistic art historians to supply.

For the art of the mid-fourth century it is more important to ask whether Aristotle established transferable criteria when he defined tragedy. Tragedy existed and was popular. How could it be defended from the attacks which Plato had made in the *Republic*?

In the first place 'imitation' is not a method of reproducing copies three times removed from the original Idea (which was Plato's objection), but a fundamental and distinctive human activity, which is a valid method of obtaining knowledge; this defence is as applicable to illusionistic painting as to realistic tragedy. Secondly, the arousing of passion, which Plato so much deplored, is accepted as the end of tragedy and justified as a katharsis (whatever that may mean). To this end tragedy must be an organic composition of interrelated scenes with a hero of a status that awakes our pity and fear, and with incidents, such as surprises and recognitions, which excite the maximum of emotion in the audience.

That tragedy in the mid-fourth century emphasised emotion more than in the fifth century is clear also from the masks (*91*). A number of reliefs and paintings of tragic masks show that both on men's and women's faces the emotion is stressed by furrowed foreheads to show grief, brows arched to show pride or anger, flaring nostrils to show scorn, and brows sloping downward from the nose to show distress. The mask could not, of course, show change of emotion (except in comedy, where masks with one gloomy and one cheerful side were sometimes used) so that they were presumably chosen to fit the most important scene that the actor had to play. The emotional effect is still more enhanced by the tower of hair over the forehead on the so-called onkos masks introduced in Athens about 330 and thereafter normal in the Hellenistic age (*49*).

Whether Plato would have accepted Aristotle's defence of tragedy as adequate is doubtful. In the *Laws* he still regards tragedy as mob-rhetoric, which should not be allowed in the well-governed city, and there is no sign that he changed his standpoint. The new emotional rhetoric, best known to us from the speeches of Demosthenes and Aeschines, he had to accept as part of the political world in which he wished his students to be effective. Illusionistic painting he had attacked in the *Republic* primarily because he was using it as a parallel phenomenon to realistic tragedy, which was the main object

91 Tragic actor with mask

92   Psyche, golden ear-ring

of his censure. But, if my interpretation is right, he swiftly recognised the claim of the Sikyonian painters that they were making an orderly arrangement of mutually adapted parts.

In this period the myth of the *Phaedrus* (247c) asks for explanation in terms of art. There the winged charioteer of the immortal soul after the greatest struggles and labours catches at most a glimpse of Justice herself, Modesty herself and Knowledge herself in the 'place beyond heaven' where they dwell; the gods can see them when they will. The abstract ideas in their place beyond heaven remind us again of the picture of Herakles in the garden of the Hesperides, a subject which was also common in the fourth century. And the perilous chariot-drive of the immortal soul recalls the many pictures of the young Herakles driving to heaven in the chariot of Athena (see fig. *53*). Thus Plato clothes his thought in forms which we know from the art of his youth and early middle age; perhaps he also influenced the artists.

It has been suggested that a very beautiful pair of ear-rings was inspired by the chariot-drive of the soul in the *Phaedrus* (*92*). A winged girl is driving a two-horsed chariot upwards to an elaborate floral ornament, which may represent the 'place beyond heaven'; the winged girl is Psyche, the soul. Another pair of ear-rings, which comes from near Salonika in ancient Macedonia, has Ganymede carried by the eagle towards a similar floral ornament. The eagle carried Ganymede up to Zeus to be his cupbearer, so that the interpretation of the floral ornament on both these pairs of ear-rings as heaven seems justifiable. Then Ganymede's rise to heaven may be a symbol of the journey of the soul.

In so far as it is possible to realise Plato's conception of the gods in plastic form the Athenian sculptor Praxiteles comes near to doing it. What characterises Praxiteles' gods is their bliss, perfection and detachment, and these are the qualities which Plato ascribes to the divine. The Hermes at Olympia (93), the Aphrodite of Knidos and the Apollo Sauroktonos (lizard-slaying) give us some idea of his compositions and, if not of his style in detail, at least of his intentions. All three compositions are meant to be seen from a single view-point: the vertical of the main figure is balanced by another vertical—tree-trunk for the Apollo, tree-trunk and drapery for Hermes, drapery and hydria for Aphrodite. In all three the vertical of the human figure is resolved in a series of subtle and balancing curves which contrasts with the more formal vertical of the support. All three are engaged in what they are doing and have no glance for the spectator; Apollo looks at the lizard, Hermes at the baby Dionysos, Aphrodite looks into the distance. They live in a detached world of youth and bliss.

A bronze original, the boy found in the sea off Marathon (94), seems by the fineness and delicacy of its workmanship to claim a close kinship with Praxiteles. If his right hand held a twig on a trunk the whole would make the same sort of contrast between stiff vertical and flowing lines of body and limbs that is so satisfactory in the Apollo. This may have been a young Hermes; what he was looking at so carefully in his left hand we cannot tell. The execution is exquisite, and the preservation of the eyes makes it possible for us to recapture a great deal of the charm of the figure.

Praxiteles did not only make

93   Hermes of Praxiteles,
Olympia

94 Bronze boy from
Marathon

gods and heroes, and his sons carried his tradition on into the early third century. Stylistically the charming terracotta figures, known as Tanagras, because so many of them were found in the tombs of the small town of Tanagra across the border in Boeotia, have always seemed to have a close connection with Praxiteles and his sons. Now the connection has been clearly established by the discovery of similar figures in the Athenian Agora. An attractive little lady (*95*) with a wreath in her left hand and the popular coiffure known as melon hair was found in the dump of a terracotta-maker's workshop in the Athenian Agora (p. 58). She can be dated 350–340 and therefore in Praxiteles' lifetime. She has had her hair done carefully, and she has put on her best frock, perhaps because she is going to walk in procession like the girls of the Parthenon frieze, to lay her wreath on the altar of a goddess.

Praxiteles and his sons continue right through the fourth century what is essentially a modification of the rather sweet style of the Nike balustrade. They are only moderately affected by the revolution to which the *Phaedrus* and the *Poetics* testify. In the *Poetics*, as we have seen, Aristotle is aware all the time of art as a parallel activity to poetry; both are imitative, a parallel history of both is possible, and when he demands organic composition of a certain size and scale for poetry, he illustrates what he means by referring to painting.

Composition was the strong point of the Sikyonian school, and the Sikyonian painter Pamphilos evidently placed a new emphasis on drawing. When we read this against our knowledge of the rich

178

style, it seems to be the messy outlines of the Meidias painter and his successors that prompted this reaction, and Plato's criticisms of skiagraphia in the *Republic* rather suggest that in big painting also realism achieved by colour and shading may have been sometimes purchased at the expense of clear outlines and composition. Pamphilos certainly could not put back the clock; perspective and shading had come to stay; but he could and probably did subordinate perspective and shading to drawing and composition. In Athens the new clean strong style of vase-painting, which is called the Kerch style because so many examples have been found in south Russia, has naturally been thought to show his influence: the symposion scene discussed above (p. 37) is an early instance.

Pamphilos had a pupil called Pausias, who was an expert in the technique of encaustic, painting with hot wax, which was the ancient equivalent of oils. Possibly because he was primarily interested in exploiting technique he painted among other things small pictures of flowers. He obviously *was* interested in technique because he painted an ox seen from behind so that the modelling of different tones of black showed the solidity of the animal, and he painted a picture of Methe (personification of drunkenness) drinking from a glass cup so that her face could be seen through the glass.

Pausias was criticised by his younger contemporary Nikias of Athens for carving up his art into small subjects like birds and flowers. Pausias is not named, but he must surely be the object of this remark. One should choose a large subject like a cavalry-battle or a sea-battle. Nikias was the painter whom Praxiteles thought the most skilful at colouring his statues. His Andromeda is known from copies in Pompeii and certainly has size in the sense that the figures are large for their frame. Nikias was the pupil of a scarcely known Antidotos, and Antidotos was the pupil of Euphranor. The difference in age between Euphranor and Nikias need not have been great; they both represented Alexander, and Euphranor also painted in the Stoa of Zeus Eleutherios at Athens (see above

95 Attic
terracotta
statuette

p. 64) the battle of Mantineia, which took place in 362 BC, and that picture was a cavalry-battle, one of the subjects approved by Nikias.

Euphranor of the Isthmus was both painter and sculptor. According to Pliny 'he seems to have been the first to express the nobility of heroes'. The 'dignity of heroes' clearly could be shown by size; and Euphranor claimed that his Theseus was fed on beef whereas Parrhasios' Theseus was fed on roses. The contrast can be seen by comparing Herakles on fourth-century vases with the Herakles of the Meidias painter (pp. 110, 112). In a rather different sense Euphranor preserved the 'dignity of heroes' by not showing that Hephaistos was lame, just as the contemporary tragic poet Theodektes avoided making Philoctetes lame by transferring the snake-bite to his hand. Plato presumably approved of this desire to preserve heroic dignity.

96   Apollo Patroos

Besides the cavalry-battle of Mantineia, in which Xenophon's son Grylos and the Boeotian general Epameinondas were included, Euphranor painted, also in the Stoa of Zeus Eleutherios, a picture of the Twelve Gods (presumably his Hephaistos was one of them) and a picture of Theseus, Democracy, and Demos. This was presumably the beef-fed Theseus. According to Pausanias the painting showed that Theseus established equality of political rights for the Athenians. Theseus, as we have seen, had been the hero of the Athenian democracy since the late sixth century. In 339 Isokrates said that Theseus had

97   Apollo and Marsyas

handed over the city to the people to rule. Certainly Democracy
and Demos are personifications, and the whole picture was a
political allegory to show that democracy was the ancestral
Athenian constitution. The three pictures together celebrated the
peace achieved for the moment by the battle of Mantineia, a
battle won with the will of the Olympian gods (the Twelve Gods)
and by the virtue of the Athenian democracy. If Theseus was
giving Democracy to Demos, he was probably giving her to Demos
as a bride.

Next to the Stoa of Zeus on the west side of the Agora is the
Temple of Apollo Patroos (p. 64). The temple was built in the
third quarter of the fourth century over the remains of an earlier
temple of the mid-sixth century. The cult-statue for the new temple
was made by Euphranor and has been identified with the remains
of a colossal statue found 20 yards to the south of the temple (96).
Apollo is striding forward playing his lyre. He wears a long chiton
down to his feet and the overfall is belted round his waist. Within
the heavy folds, which give the main verticals, the artist has enjoyed
the little crinkly folds below the belt and over both the feet.

The whole figure inspired a vase-painter who wanted an Apollo
for a Marsyas scene (97). The satyr Marsyas, after having tried the

98   Grave-relief: Aristonautes

flute discarded by Athena, challenged Apollo to a musical competition and was defeated and flayed. In this picture Apollo dominates the scene. His mother Leto is above on the left. Victory flies between her and Apollo. His sister Artemis is above on the right. Marsyas sits on a rock listening hopelessly; his flutes have fallen from his hand. Marsyas' pupil, Olympos, reclines on the left, succumbing completely to Apollo's music. Apollo wears the long sleeves of the professional musician; his left arm passes through the band at the back of the concert lyre so that his fingers can stop the strings; his right hand holds the plektron (with which the strings are plucked); his long hair is bound by a golden bay wreath. This composition of large solemn figures grouped round a single figure, who dominates them emotionally by his performance, illustrates what Aristotle means by an organic composition designed to arouse emotion.

The two factors in vases of this time which give them their emotional effect are the scale of the figures and their frontality: they look out of their frames at the spectator. This we can see also in sculpture of the time. The grave-relief of Aristonautes (98) translates the dreamy, inspired movement of Apollo into energetic action, but the pose is essentially the same. The left hand with the shield grip and rim of the shield, and the right hand with the sword have been broken away. Aristonautes is moving rapidly towards the right but he turns to watch an enemy coming from the left, and so he looks out of his framework at us. What is new in these mid-fourth-century grave-reliefs is again the scale of the figure in relation to the frame and the frontality, and also the depth of the little temple in which they are set.

The emotion of the face is due largely to the deep-sinking of the inner corners of the eyes associated sometimes with very fleshy overhanging eyebrows. This can be seen also in an original marble statue of about 330, the Demeter of Knidos in the British Museum (99). The justification for including it here is that although two very different sculptors have been suggested for it, Leochares and Bryaxis, they were both in fact Athenian. The treatment of the drapery with the heavy nearly horizontal lines across the breast is typical of the period. This is Demeter grieving for her daughter, as in the Eleusinian story. The precinct where the Demeter was found was sacred to Persephone (Kore) as well as Demeter, and therefore it is extremely likely that a figure of Kore stood beside her mother, and a terracotta statuette found in the precinct probably gives the type. Unfortunately we know nothing of how the two statues were framed: at least one would suppose that the Demeter was nearly frontal. She has no Praxitelean detachment, but communicates her sorrow direct to the spectator.

The justification for grouping all these works together under the general heading, Late Classical Style, is that, in spite of their many and obvious differences, they have the common quality of good composition and clear outlines. And this common quality justifies the name classical; it is the quality which these works share with the classical works of the third quarter of the fifth century. What distinguishes them from the classical works of the Parthenon period is largely the technical advances made in the intervening Free Period, which have now become part of every artist's stock in trade: perspective and shading in painting,

99   Demeter of Knidos

the means of representing emotion both in painting and sculpture, the use of much higher relief and more complicated poses in sculpture. There is also a change of approach. It would be an over-simplification to say that classical composition is used to restrain emotion and late classical composition is used to communicate it, but this simplification explains something of the change. The experience is more directly communicated now, the range of experience communicated is greater, and the experience communicated by the particular work is more individual and personal.

This is part of a more general change, which manifests itself also in literature, in the philosophers and in the orators, in tragedy also, as we know from the masks; in comedy there is a complete revolution—political satire, fantasy, parody and obscenity give place to social comedy, as we know it today. This change in comedy is gradual: love stories probably came in first as parodies of tragedy, then they needed new characters, the intriguing slave, the parasite, and the procurer; Aristotle already talks of 'chance names' (as distinct from the historical characters of Old Comedy) and a sequence of probable incidents in comedy; then, just after our period, with Menander the abandonment of the old obscene costume made the characters look as if they belonged to upper-class Athenian households, and social comedy started its long career through Plautus, Molière, Shakespeare, to our own day. The problems of the young lover in upper-class Athenian house-holds were not very different from the problems of the young in upper-class households of any place or time, and Menander's humane and civilised treatment produced a kind of drama which could be exported over the widening Greek world of the Hellenistic age and translated or adapted for successive generations down to T. S. Eliot's *Confidential Clerk* and beyond.

One other factor in this general change should be mentioned, re-spect for the great Greek past: when we think of the ruthlessness with which archaic statues were used for raising the level of the Acropolis in 480, the rapid progress of Greek art from the seventh to the fifth century, or the complete modernisation of Homeric heroes in Greek tragedy, conscious respect for the past, as distinct from the occasional conservatism of the artist or writer who continues in the old manner, is the last thing we should attribute to the Greeks, but we have seen signs of it growing from the late fifth century—occasional archaism in painting and sculpture,

Aristophanes' rejuvenated Demos 'shining in his ancient dress', the respect for the old Athenian democracy in Demosthenes, Isokrates and Plato, the annual revival of a fifth-century tragedy through the fourth century, the beginning of historical scholarship in Aristotle. For the future this was a potent force to which we owe the preservation of classical texts through Hellenistic and Roman scholarship and, to some extent, the preservation of classical art through Hellenistic and Roman adaptations and copies. Respect for the past for a Greek meant also belief in man as a rational animal who can solve his own problems and live with his neighbours, a belief which survived in spite of the flamboyance and violence of the Hellenistic kings.

BOOKS FOR FURTHER READING

CHAPTER I

C. W. J. Eliot, *Coastal Demes of Attika*, Toronto, 1962
A. Andrewes, *The Greeks*, Hutchinson, 1967, Chapters 1 and 4
N. G. L. Hammond, *History of Greece to 322 B.C.*, Oxford, 1959
J. S. Morrison, *Notes on certain Greek nautical terms*, Classical Quarterly, 41, 1947, 122
R. J. Hopper, *The Mines and Miners of Ancient Athens*, Greece and Rome, 8, 1961, 138
C. J. K. Cunningham, *The Silver of Laurion*, Greece and Rome, 14, 1967, 145

CHAPTER II

R. E. Wycherley, *How the Greeks built cities*, Macmillan, 1949, Ch.7, Greek Houses
T. B. L. Webster, *Houses: Inside and Outside*, Bulletin of the John Rylands Library, 45, 1962, 253
W. K. Pritchett and D. A. Amyx, *The Attic Stelai*, Hesperia, 22, 1953, 225; 24, 1956, 178; 27, 1958, 168
H. A. Thompson, *The Athenian Agora*, 1962, 112, 116
J. E. Jones etc., *The Dema House in Attica*, Annual of the British School at Athens, 57, 1962, 75ff.
A. French, *The Growth of the Athenian Economy*, Routledge and Kegan Paul, 1964
A. Andrewes, *The Greeks*, Chs. 6 and 7
V. Ehrenberg, *The People of Aristophanes*, Blackwell, 1951, Chs. 3 and 7
R. M. Cook, *Greek Painted Pottery*, Methuen, 1960
B. A. Sparkes and L. Talcott, *Pots and Pans of Classical Athens*, American School of Classical Studies, Princeton N.J., 1958

J. Perlzweig, *Lamps from the Athenian Agora*, American School of Classical Studies, Princeton N. J., 1963

E. N. Gardiner, *Athletics of the Ancient World*, Oxford, 1930

H. I. Marrou, *A History of Education in Antiquity*, Sheed and Ward

R. E. Wycherley, *Peripatos: the Athenian Philosophical Scene*, Greece and Rome, 8, 1961, 153; 9, 1962, 2

CHAPTER III

H. A. Thompson, *The Athenian Agora*, 1962

R. E. Wycherley, *How the Greeks built cities*, Ch. 4

The Market of Athens, Greece and Rome, 3, 1956, 2

The Athenian Agora III, Literary and epigraphical testimonia, American School of Classical Studies, Princeton, N.J., 1957

A. Andrewes, *The Greeks*, Ch. 9

V. Ehrenberg, *The People of Aristophanes*, Chs. 5 and 13

The Greek State, Blackwell, 1960, Ch. 2

A. H. M. Jones, *Athenian democracy*, Blackwell, 1957

CHAPTER IV

A. Andrewes, *The Greeks*, Ch. 11

W. K. C. Guthrie, *The Greeks and their gods*, Methuen, 1950

M. P. Nilsson, *Greek Piety*, Oxford, 1948

H. W. Parke, *Greek Oracles*, Hutchinson, 1967

A. E. Raubitschek, *Dedications from the Athenian Acropolis*, Princeton, 1949

G. E. Mylonas, *Eleusis and the Eleusinian Mysteries*, Eleusis, 1961

C. J. Herington, *Athena Parthenos and Athena Polias*, Manchester, 1955

A. W. Pickard-Cambridge, *The Dramatic Festivals of Athens*, Oxford, 1953

T. B. L. Webster, *Staging and Scenery in the Ancient Theatre*, Bulletin of the John Rylands Library, 42, 1960, 493

CHAPTER V

H. J. Rose, *Handbook of Greek Mythology*, Methuen, 1964

T. B. L. Webster, *The Myth of Ariadne from Homer to Catullus*, Greece and Rome, 13, 1966, 22

Stesichoros: Geryoneis, Agon 2, 1968

H. Lloyd-Jones, *Heracles at Eleusis*, Maia 3, 1967, 206

M. Ostwald, *Pinder, Nomos, and Heracles*, Harvard Studies in Classical Philology, 69, 1965, 109

Gilbert Murray, *Greek Studies*, Oxford, 1946, Ch. 7

CHAPTER VI

A. Lesky, *History of Greek Literature*, Methuen, 1966, Book V

G. M. A. Richter, *A Handbook of Greek Art*, Phaidon, 1959

J. D. Beazley and B. Ashmole, *Greek Sculpture and Painting*, Cambridge, 1966

J. Barron, *Greek Sculpture*, Dutton Vista, 1965

P. Devambez, *Greek Painting*, Weidenfeld and Nicolson, 1962

B. Ashmole and N. Yalouris, *Olympia*, Phaidon, 1967

P. E. Corbett, *The Sculpture of the Parthenon*, Penguin, 1959

E. B. Harrison, *The East pediment of the Parthenon*, American Journal of Archaeology, 71, 1967, 27

E. B. Harrison, *New Sculpture from the Athenian Agora*, Hesperia, 29, 1960, 369

J. R. Green, *A New Oinochoe Series*, Hesperia, 31, 1962, 82

Rhys Carpenter, *Sculpture of the Nike Temple Parapet*, Harvard, 1929

H. Friis Johansen, *The Attic Grave Reliefs*, Copenhagen, 1951

A. Rumpf, *Parrhasios*, American Journal of Archaeology, 55, 1951, 1

T. B. L. Webster, *Art and Literature in fourth century Athens*, London, 1956

D. B. Thompson, *The Origin of Tanagras*, American Journal of Archaeology, 70, 1966, 51

The Society for Promotion of Hellenic Studies (31–34 Gordon Square, W.C.1) publishes 'Archaeological Reports' with pictures annually; these can be obtained by anyone from the Society at the price of 12s. 6d. A subscription to the Society of £3 per annum entitles the member to receive 'Archaeological Reports' and the 'Journal of Hellenic Studies', to attend the Society's meetings, and to use its Library and Slide-Collection.

INDEX

The figures in **bold type** refer to the figure numbers of the illustrations